The Heart of Teachir

The Heart of Teaching is a book about teaching and learning in the performing arts. Its focus is on the inner dynamics of teaching: the processes by which teachers can promote—or undermine—creativity itself. It covers many of the issues that teachers, directors, and choreographers experience, from the frustrations of dealing with silent students, and helping young artists "unlearn" their inhibitions, to problems of resistance, judgment, and race in the classroom.

Wangh raises questions about what can—and what cannot—be taught, and opens a discussion about the social, psychological, and spiritual values that underlie the skills and techniques that teachers impart. Subjects addressed include:

- Question asking: which kinds of questions encourage creativity and which can subvert the learning process;
- Feedback: how it can foster either dependence or independence in students;
- Grading: its meaning and meaninglessness;
- Power relationships, transference and counter-transference;
- The pivotal role of listening.

The Heart of Teaching speaks to both experienced and beginning teachers in all disciplines, but is of specific relevance to those in the performing arts, from which most of its examples are drawn. This book brings essential insights and honesty to the discussion of how teachers really interact with students.

Stephen Wangh is a playwright, director and acting teacher. He has taught at Emerson College, New York University, Naropa University, and the Lasalle College of the Arts, Singapore. He is the author of 15 plays and co-writer of *The People's Temple* and *The Laramie Project*. He is the author of *An Acrobat of the Heart: A Physical Approach to Acting Inspired by the Work of Jerzy Grotowski*.

The Heart of Teaching

Empowering Students in the Performing Arts

Stephen Wangh

Routledge
Taylor & Francis Group

LONDON AND NEW YORK

First published 2013
by Routledge
2 Park Square, Milton Park, Abingdon, Oxon OX14 4RN

Simultaneously published in the USA and Canada
by Routledge
711 Third Avenue, New York, NY 10017

Routledge is an imprint of the Taylor & Francis Group, an informa business

British Library Cataloguing in Publication Data
A catalogue record for this book is available from the British Library

Library of Congress Cataloguing in Publication Data
Wangh, Stephen.
Heart of teaching : empowering students in the performing
arts / Stephen Wangh.
p. cm.
Includes bibliographical references and index.
1. Performing arts--Study and teaching. I. Title.
PN1576.W36 2012
790.2071--dc23
2012028659

ISBN: 978-0-415-64491-4 (hbk)
ISBN: 978-0-415-64492-1 (pbk)
ISBN: 978-0-203-07588-3 (ebk)

Typeset in Sabon
by Taylor & Francis Books

Printed and bound in Great Britain by the MPG Books Group

For Noah and Hannah

The courage to teach is the courage to keep one's heart open in those very moments when the heart is asked to hold more than it is able.

Parker J. Palmer

Be patient toward all that is unsolved in your heart and try to love the questions themselves.

Rainer Maria Rilke

Contents

Acknowledgements

All through the four-year-long journey of writing this book, Suzanne Baxtresser has been my first and last reader, my Secure Partner, and my moral and physical support. To her, great gratitude is due. I am also especially indebted to Chris Rohmann, Angela Delichatsios, and Pam Rickard, who read the manuscript at various stages along the way, and whose suggestions for cuts and clarifications were helpful beyond measure. Thanks also to Paul Binnerts, Paul Langland, Terry Knickerbocker, Chaunesti Webb, and Anne Bernstein for their input, and to Wendell Beavers for allowing me to learn what teaching about teaching might entail. Special thanks go to Ben Piggott, whose steady editorial hand guided me towards many felicitous changes during the final leg of this trip.

Most of all: thanks to the hard-working, inquisitive, feisty, caring students who taught me everything I know about teaching.

Extracts from *The Courage to Teach: Exploring the Inner Landscape of a Teacher's Life* by Parker J. Palmer (Copyright © 1997 Parker J. Palmer). Reproduced by permission of John Wiley and Sons Inc.

Extracts from *A Soprano on her Head* by Eloise Ristad (1982). Reproduced by permission of Real People Press.

Preface

During the summer of 2003, I led a workshop in physical acting for high school and college acting teachers. My book, *An Acrobat of the Heart: A Physical Approach to Acting Inspired by the Work of Jerzy Grotowski*, had been published three years earlier, and during the following years I had heard anecdotally that acting teachers in colleges and high schools had begun teaching their students some of the exercises in the book. I found these stories encouraging; they meant that the work was spreading. But I also found them a little unsettling because that book had been written for actors, not for teachers, and it did not say anything about how to teach the work.

In fact, my early drafts of *An Acrobat of the Heart* had included several short passages describing why I had responded to a student in a certain way or, conversely, why I had withheld my perceptions about what I'd just seen during an exercise. But as I rewrote that manuscript, I had removed all those teacherly thoughts. It had seemed to me that they read like asides, whispers between one teacher and another, private comments that would be distractions for someone who was reading the book from an actor's point of view.

So the summer 2003 workshop with teachers was my first attempt to see if I could pass along not only *what* I was teaching, but also *how* I went about teaching it. I set out to lead the workshop just as I always taught, simply allowing some extra time at the end of each class to answer any pedagogical questions my teacher-students might have about the exercises we'd done. As always, I began by teaching the warm-up lessons that help students create a safe working space. Then I taught the physical training exercises that I'd learned from Jerzy Grotowski in 1967. During the second week of the workshop, I had each of the students bring in a dramatic monologue so that they could experience how Grotowski's work could be applied to text-based performance. After each monologue presentation, before I shared any of my own impressions,

I asked each student to take a moment to tell us about her own experience: which particular moments she'd liked, which lines, gestures, images had seemed useful and appropriate during her performance. And sometimes, if the student started to talk instead about what had gone *wrong* for her, I'd steer her attention back toward the positive observations she could make. Then, when she had finished, I would speak about what I'd seen, and we'd spend a few minutes working through parts of the monologue. There was nothing special about this teaching progression; it was just what I'd been doing in my acting classes for years.

But one day, after the last monologue had been worked on, one of the participants in the workshop remarked: "I've always assumed that after a student shows a scene, I should put my attention on what is *not* working. It was a revelation to me that you began with what *is* working. Why do you do that?"

As I began to answer her question, I realized that, in fact, there were a great many reasons why I processed the students' work in the way I did; reasons that had to do with the teacher–student relationship. Reasons that had to do with how learning happens. Reasons that had to do with empowerment, and with my views of what education is actually about. Many too many thoughts to share at that moment—enough to start me wondering why I hadn't been aware of these thoughts before.

The *hows* of teaching

The physical approach to acting I studied with the Polish director Jerzy Grotowski had been life-changing for me. Although the 1967 workshop in which I studied with him had lasted only four weeks, I spent the next 30 years devising ways to pass that work along, trying to help American acting students (re)discover how to use their bodies as dynamic sources for their acting. Over the years, many of the students who attended my acting classes had told me that this physical approach to acting had reawakened their enthusiasm for performing, an enthusiasm that they felt had been stifled by other, more cerebral training systems.

During those 30 years I had worked on ways of making Grotowski's work accessible to American actors, and had been so caught up in my fascination with the work itself that I hadn't noticed that, along the way, I had also developed a *way* of teaching, a style of responding to students and giving feedback, a facility for dealing with difficult students—and some definite opinions about *why* I taught the way I did. And once I stopped to think about the *whys* and *hows* of my teaching, instead of just about *what* I taught, it occurred to me that these questions of *why* and *how* might be relevant not only to teachers of acting but to anyone who was teaching or directing performers. Moreover, I became aware that one reason I had remained so oblivious to my own thoughts and opinions about the teaching process for so long was that these were subjects that I had never dared to discuss with my colleagues.

When we teachers met in the Teacher Lounge at the Experimental Theatre Wing at NYU, we might complain to one another about our most obstreperous students. We might talk about our battles with administrators, and occasionally we might even argue the pros and cons of different acting or movement techniques. But we seldom mentioned the *hows* of teaching. We never talked about things such as how we answered or avoided answering students' questions. We might compare notes on a student whose behavior we found difficult, but we wouldn't say, "His way of joking really pushes my buttons." And we certainly never confessed to each other when we found ourselves infatuated with someone in our class. Perhaps we feared that talking about such things would expose us to others' judgments, perhaps we felt these subjects were private concerns we ought to be able to deal with on our own. But as I thought about it, I wondered if these sorts of discussions were somehow taboo.

Then, after the summer workshop in 2003, I began to wonder if other teachers also worried about such things, if others felt the same frustrations I did, or held strong opinions about these kinds of things. I wondered if they, like me, were often unaware of why they taught as they did. And I wondered what we all might learn from each other if we talked with each other about what *really* transpired between ourselves and our students, if we discussed the frustrations, the obsessions, and the loneliness of the long-distance teacher.

Allowing myself to contemplate the ups and downs I went through as a teacher, I became acutely aware that, even after all these years in classrooms and studios, there were ways in which being a teacher remained problematic for me. There were still some students who stumped me, frustrated me, or made me question my ability as a teacher, and there were still days when I "took my work home with me" after things had gone badly in my acting classes.

I also became more aware that during the past couple of years I had allowed myself to give teaching advice to some of the younger teachers. And now I began to wonder: Who was I to give other teachers advice? After all, I myself had never studied teaching. Like many teachers of performance, I was just an artist who had realized that, in order to survive, he was going to need a day-job.

So, setting out to write on a subject I'd never studied, I felt I ought to see if perhaps other teachers had already written everything that needed to be said on the subject. And indeed, I discovered that there were many library shelves loaded down with books on pedagogy. There were books on cognitive and educational psychology, books on feminist pedagogy, on multicultural curricular reform, on "constructivist learning," and "problem-based learning." The majority of these books were about teaching in elementary or high schools, and most of the books about teaching on the college level were written by teachers of literature, with a few by teachers in the sciences. But the books about teaching in the performing arts dealt mostly with topics such as "multiple intelligences," and how to encourage creativity in the classroom.[1] With the notable exception of Eloise Ristad's wonderful *A Soprano on Her Head*, the books about teaching performers all seemed to be about *what* we teach—craft and technique—rather than about *how*—the dynamics of what actually happens in the classroom between teacher and student.

I did come across several books—most of them by literature teachers in the Quaker tradition—that discussed the problems that fascinated me: the strange, terrifying, and wondrous dance that teachers and students perform with each other; the paradoxes surrounding the power we teachers wield; and the strange mixture of joy and heartbreak that teaching can engender. So, in writing the chapters that follow, I have allowed myself to quote liberally from authors such as Parker Palmer and Anne French Dalke.

The purpose of this book is to open a discussion among teachers of performance and of other disciplines, about the joys, the fears, and the unspoken (unspeakable?) travails of teaching. My hope is that teachers and other artists—theater directors and choreographers, for instance—will find some of what I say applies to their work too. Since I've now spent nearly 40 years teaching physical acting, the majority of the stories I recount are based upon events I've experienced in actor-training classes. But I've made an effort to steer clear of questions of *what we teach* to concentrate instead on questions of *how we teach*, the kinds of questions that all teachers of performance, of acting, movement, voice, and music—and perhaps teachers of other disciplines—might encounter. Issues such as:

- What are we really teaching while we teach technique?
- How do we ask and answer questions?

1 "Multiple intelligence" refers to the idea that what we call IQ is not the only measure of intelligence. For instance, some people have a greater capacity for understanding emotions than others do. For more, see Daniel Goleman (1995) *Emotional Intelligence* (Bantam, NY) and Howard Gardner (1993) *Multiple Intelligences: The Theory in Practice* (Basic Books, NY). For an overview of the literature on creativity, see Ruth Richards (ed.) (2007) *Everyday Creativity and New Views of Human Nature* (American Psychological Association, Washington DC).

- How do we listen, or fail to listen, to our students?
- How do we give our students feedback?
- How do we become entangled in fearing or loving or hating our students?
- How do we wield or conceal the power we have?
- And how can we cultivate the endurance that teaching requires?

Most of what I say in this book is based on personal experience. The majority of the stories I tell are true, though the names have been changed and some of the details have been fictionalized or conflated from several incidents. But please note: I haven't written this book because I think I know the answers to all the questions I raise here, or because I think I've identified all the important issues. I've written it in the hope of opening a space in which teachers—and performers and directors—might consider their own opinions on these and similar issues, and discuss them with each other.

A note to beginning teachers

Just as there is no book that can teach you how to swim, there is also no book that can teach you how to teach. As with swimming, there is no way to learn teaching without getting wet. When you begin, you may feel a need to enter the classroom or studio with lots of plans and exercises in mind. But as time goes on, you will probably discover that teaching is often less about the lesson-plans and more about simply being there for and with your students, listening to them and responding to what they seem to need today. And that is true not only in the arts.

> When people first learn I am a teacher, they generally ask what I teach. And, for many years, I always answered, "biochemistry." But recently I overheard another answer to this question, one that was more interesting. So now when people ask what I teach, I use that answer. I say, "I teach students."
>
> (Zull, 2002, p. 222)

Teaching is a strange activity, simultaneously public and lonesome. Every day a teacher works surrounded by her students, and yet is totally alone. But I encourage you to find mentors, to ask questions of other teachers, and to talk about your experiences with others. You'll find you're not alone in your loneliness.

Introduction

What teachers don't talk about

The first acting class I ever taught was to a group of teenagers in Brooklyn during the fall of 1969. These were kids who had watched the plays that our street theater company, The New York Free Theater, had performed in Park Slope the previous summer. Our shows were musicals about racism and drugs and money, shows that we hoped would inspire our audiences to challenge the powers that be and change the world. Instead, what we found was that those teenagers who came back day after day to see what we were doing were more interested in learning how to make theater than in how to overthrow the state. So we decided to teach them to make their own plays.

I was 25 and fresh out of graduate school. I had never taught acting or playmaking before, but I figured I could remember the exercises my teachers had taught. I'd directed shows, and as a kid I'd always enjoyed telling my younger brothers how to perform. What did I have to lose? It turned out that what I had to lose was my innocence about teaching.

The students were wonderful: enthusiastic, eager to learn, and willing to do any exercise I proposed. Moreover, I found my thoughts wandering to one of the girls in the group, who wore beautiful peasant blouses, and who often gazed at me—or so I imagined—in such a soulful way ... . Their enthusiasm for the work helped me overcome my doubts, so, on the long Wednesday evening subway rides to Brooklyn, I cobbled together a few acting exercises I remembered from my own training and hoped that they would lead us somewhere. But then one Wednesday, I discovered that teaching might require something more than that. I had decided to teach a developmental exercise I'd learned in an acting class several years before. I vaguely remembered that we'd begun lying on the floor and slowly grown from small seeds into giant trees. I decided to alter the exercise a little and have these young actors grow from birth into human beings. After our warm-up tag game, I had the class lie down on the floor, and I talked them through a relaxation and then into some guided imagery:

"Imagine that when you open your eyes, you've just been born, and you are seeing the world for the first time." I spoke in a soft voice, gently urging them to discover sight and movement as if they were infants. Soon they were all crawling around the floor of the church basement like ten-month-old babies. To my delight, the exercise was working! They looked like they were having great fun, babbling and cooing as if they didn't speak a word. When I suggested they try crying or laughing, they did it. If I asked them to notice the other babies, they did that too. My God, I thought, these kids would do anything I asked. Cool. But after a few minutes, I realized I had no idea where to take this exercise. Should we develop characters? What characters? We didn't have any text. What was this exercise about anyway? I realized I didn't know. My teenage charges were happily crawling around, trusting that their teacher knew what the hell he was doing. But in fact, I had no idea what to do next, so I decided to just drop the exercise and move on to some fun theater games.

"Good," I said to the babbling babies, "that was fine, but now we're going to let that go. Everybody stand up!"

The kids looked around a bit, but they all kept crawling.

"Okay," I said, "that's over, now. We're going to go on to another exercise." More crawling. The girl in the peasant blouse was staring up at me from the floor as if she were entirely lost. None of them seemed to understand me, or was it that they didn't know how to stand?

It began to dawn on me that somehow these teenagers had become hypnotized by my voice. But now, when I tried snapping my fingers, clapping my hands, or calling their names, nothing seemed to work. I had become a Sorcerer's Apprentice with no idea how to end the spell. In desperation, I resumed the calm, soft voice I'd used at the start of the exercise.

"Okay, you're getting tired of crawling now. Lie down; it's time to go to bed. You're very tired. Close your eyes. Good. That's good. Now when you wake up, you'll all be back here in the church basement. And you'll be your real ages again, okay?" I kept my voice soothing, but inside my head, my mind was racing. What could I do? Whom could I call? What would I say to the police?

Thankfully, my calming words worked, more or less. After a few minutes, the kids sat up and were able to talk, though they still looked a little dazed. But I, myself, was more than a little shaken. I let the kids talk for a while about the exercise—long enough to satisfy myself that they had, indeed, recovered. In fact, they all seemed to have had a good time "playing at" being babies, so I brought the class to a quick finish, and sent the kids home, hoping they would remember where they lived. This time, on my long subway ride back to Manhattan, I had a great deal more to think about than my preoccupation with a high school girl. What the hell had happened? What had I done? And why hadn't anyone told me that teaching could go wrong like this?

It was only many years later that I realized I'd managed to founder upon two of the great hazards of teaching: the mysteries of Transference and the dangers of oblivious Power. And the reason no one had told me was ... I'd never asked.

But whom should I have asked? No teacher in any class I'd taken had ever spoken in class about how to teach. Grade school teachers had to study education courses, but in the arts it was assumed that if you have learned a technique, you can teach it. In later years, when I applied for a job teaching acting, no one ever asked me if I'd studied teaching. If they had, I would have had to tell them that I had learned how to teach the same way the sister in the old joke learns how to swim:

"Hey buddy, how do you teach a girl how to swim?"

"Oh, teaching a girl to swim is a delicate thing, man. You have to gently put your arm around her waist and hold her hand. Then you ... "

"It's my sister."

"Oh. You throw her off the end of the dock."

The elephant in the pool

Fast forward ... 40 years.

One day two years ago, as I was starting to write this book, I went to swim laps at an indoor pool nearby, and as I turned my head to take a breath, I glanced up at the lifeguard sitting on his raised chair at the side of the pool. He was staring off into space—exactly as he had been when I'd looked up a couple of laps earlier. I wondered how he managed to stay awake. Swimming laps in a pool, I realized, is incredibly boring, but watching swimmers go back and forth for hours must be even worse. So when I finished my half-hour and pushed myself up out of the water, I walked over to the lifeguard and asked, "Does anything ever happen here? Do you ever have to save anyone?"

"No. Not in the two years I've been here. Besides, you don't want anything to ever happen."

"I'm just wondering how do you stay awake?"

"Sometimes I count the bricks on the wall. This pool is the worst. No windows, no other guards. Sometimes I realize that I've fallen asleep for like 30 seconds. It's the hardest thing."

"And when they're training you to be a lifeguard, do they give you any advice about how to stand the boredom?"

"Hell, no. They teach you how to save people. That's the job. That's supposed to be the hard part ... but it ain't."

I turned to walk toward the pool door, and then turned back to the bored lifeguard to ask one more question.

"And after you find out that the boredom is really the worst part, do you talk to other lifeguards about how to stand it?"

"Nah. Nobody talks about it. It's the ... what-d'yah-call-it. It's the elephant in the pool."

Leaving the swimming pool that day, I realized that we acting teachers are not the only ones who receive no formal training in "the hard part" of what we do, and that we are not the only ones who never talk about it. The difference, I thought, may be that some of the things teachers of performance don't talk about might be more embarrassing to discuss than the problem of boredom.

Of course, a great deal of our teaching goes swimmingly. Most students learn a great deal in our classes, and the majority of them seem to have a good time doing it. And there are many days when we feel like we know what we're doing. But this book is largely about those other days: the days when it feels as though our lesson has gotten out of hand and the moments when we wonder, "What just happened there?" It is about the students who get under our skin and the ones who don't seem like they want to learn. It is about the questions we take home with us at night, and wake up with still unanswered the next morning.

Most of the chapters in this book will explore the subtle dynamics of teacher–student interactions, unwrapping the complex ways in which even the most ephemeral moments can enhance or undermine the joys of education. But the first few chapters will consider the fundamentals of learning itself.

Chapter 1

How does learning happen?

The most beautiful thing we can experience is the mysterious. It is the source of all true art and science. He to whom this emotion is a stranger, who can no longer pause to wonder and stand rapt in awe, is as good as dead: his eyes are closed.

Albert Einstein

Let us make ourselves clear as to what the first task of education is. ... The child must learn to control his instincts. It is impossible to give him liberty to carry out all his impulses without restriction ... Accordingly, education must inhibit, forbid and suppress and this is abundantly seen in all periods of history.

Sigmund Freud

For a young child, every day is Awe-some. Learning happens at a terrific pace and every moment of learning is an experience of Wonder. When a young child paints a picture, sings a song, or plays "make-believe," the products of her artistic efforts may be ill-proportioned, off-key, or unconvincing, but her joy in the creative act is unbounded.

What happens to that sense of Wonder? I wonder.

In a recent article in *Scientific American,* neurologist Alison Gopnik suggests that there are actually two processes that interfere with this inborn human joy in learning. The first of these is the natural maturation of the human brain:

The brain region called the prefrontal cortex is distinctive to humans and takes an especially long time to mature. The adult capacities for focus, planning and efficient action that are governed by this brain area depend on the long learning that occurs in childhood. This area's wiring may not be complete until the mid-20s.

The lack of prefrontal control in young children naturally seems like a huge handicap, but it may actually be tremendously helpful for learning. The prefrontal area inhibits irrelevant thoughts and actions. But being uninhibited may help babies and young children explore freely. There is a trade-off between the ability to explore creatively and learn flexibly, like a child, and the ability to plan and act effectively like an adult. The very qualities needed to act efficiently—such as swift automatic processing and a highly pruned brain network—may be intrinsically antithetical to the qualities that are useful for learning, such as flexibility.

(Gopnik, 2010, p. 81)

Babies, Gopnik suggests, are such prodigious learners because they are uninhibited experimenters.

When children play spontaneously ("getting into everything") they are also exploring cause and effect and doing experiments—the most effective way to discover how the world works.

(Gopnik, 2010, pp. 79–80)

But soon children also begin to ask questions. One classic description of learning is the image of a six-year-old child staring up at the sky and asking her father, "Daddy, why is the sky blue?" And in this charming image one can perceive how childhood learning has already started to change. Pure Wonder has been transformed into Questioning. When she asks her father this question, the child is not asking for an explanation of how the Earth's atmosphere refracts sunlight. She has simply become aware that, if you want an adult's attention, it is more effective to ask question like, "Why is the sky blue, Daddy?" than to simply express your Awe or Wonder by exclaiming, "Look at the sky, Daddy. How blue it is!"

Wonder is a receptive state, a moment of being struck by a new phenomenon. But Questioning is Wonder that has acquired a purpose, a sort of unsatisfied Wonder in search of something, an attempt to grasp the phenomenon observed, a thirst that must be slaked with Knowledge. What has been gained in this transaction is the apprehension (in both senses) that the Unfamiliar is something to be overcome, controlled, or conquered with knowledge. What has been lost is the naïve experience of pure joy in the Unknown. It's not, of course, that there is anything bad about asking questions. The danger lies in separating intellectual comprehension from experiential sensation and in coming to accept Answers as a substitute for Awe.

In grade school, the disconnections between pure experience, thought, and action are accelerated. The six-year-old child entering first grade may jump up and down or even scream with delight when he is excited about something. But after a few months of schooling, he has learned that the appropriate physical expression for excitement—when he has something to say, for instance—is to raise his hand in the air. By the end of the year, he has learned not to jump up and down at all, though he may still wave his hand vigorously. And by the time he enters junior high school, he has learned that, no matter how eager he is to speak up, that hand should just rise, motionless, in the air rather than swinging left and right as it once did.

Perhaps the first lessons we learn about how to separate sensation and feeling from action occur even earlier, when we learn to hold on with our pelvic muscles so as not to wet our pants. Getting the hang of this inhibition, we may begin by pressing our legs together and squirming a little to the left and right. But after a few years of school, we learn that even this squirming business is improper, and that the acceptable muscular response when we have the urge to urinate is—strangely enough—exactly the same as the one for when we're excited: raising our hand. So we quietly reengineer our bodies, managing to hide all the obvious, natural signs of genito-urinary distress or intellectual enthusiasm, and we raise our hands to display the one sign that is acceptable, whether we're feeling excitement or discomfort.

Few first grade teachers would claim that hand-raising was their greatest pedagogical accomplishment—but this simple lesson probably has much longer lasting and more profound consequences upon the child than many of the lessons the teacher believes she is imparting. Nursery rhymes may fade, but hand-raising soldiers on; fortifying the disconnection between thought and action, it reinforces pelvic immobility, and it teaches the supreme importance of obeying rules. These are lessons that will reverberate for a lifetime.

Many years ago while preparing to lead a teacher-training workshop in Cuba, I saw a film about a grammar school in Canada, a film that suggested that this hand-raising business is the very core of what schooling is about. The essential lessons of primary education, the film argued, are not Reading, Writing, and 'Rithmatic, but Standing in Line, Following Orders, and Raising Your Hand. Schooling, the film argued, is purposefully designed to impart those lessons because its main function is to mold rambunctious children into compliant factory workers, submissive wives, and obedient soldiers.

I'm not sure I entirely buy this radical critique of primary education—at least not the "purposefully" part—but I do agree that one of the effects of years of schooling is to regiment minds and to disconnect those minds from their bodies, their senses, and their emotions. These disconnections are especially damaging to students in the arts.

This issue, the question of what we're really teaching while we share our expertise, will reappear in various guises throughout this book, and it is a theme we will revisit at the end.

The problem with education

We began this chapter by quoting Alison Gopnik's research showing that one of the two reasons why human beings lose their youthful enthusiasm for experimentation is the growth of the prefrontal cortex. The other reason, Gopnik says, is education itself:

> My group found that young children who think they are being instructed … may become less creative as a result. The experiment showed four-year-olds a toy that would play music if you performed the right sequence of actions on it, such as pulling a handle and then squeezing a bulb. For some children, the experimenter said: "I don't know how this toy works—let's figure it out." She proceeded to try out various longer action sequences for the children, some that ended with the short sequence and made music and some that did not. When she asked the children to make the toy work, many of them tried the correct short sequence, astutely omitting actions that were probably superfluous based on the statistics of what they had seen.
>
> With other children, the experimenter said that she would teach them how the toy worked by showing them sequences that did and did not produce music, and then she acted on the toy in exactly the same way. When asked to make the toy work, these children never tried a shortcut. Instead they mimicked the entire sequence of actions. … [The children seemed to assume] if she knew shorter sequences worked, [the teacher] would not have shown them the unnecessary actions.
>
> (Gopnik, 2010, pp. 80–81)

In other words, instruction itself can be inimical to learning!

Chapter 2

The *via negativa*

> What we usually call "developing one's talent" is often nothing more than *freeing* it from the influences that hamper, occlude and frequently destroy it entirely.
>
> Michael Chekhov

If Alison Gopnik is right, if the simple act of instructing students can undermine learning, what's left for a teacher to do? What can a teacher teach?

Many teachers will tell you that there are some things that simply cannot be taught. Talent, for instance, is something a student either has or does not have. It can't be taught. On the other hand, there are things that students can learn from a teacher: *information*, like vocabulary; *factual material*, like the history of Western Art; and *simple, practical habits*, like how to practice. These are all "teachable" matters. And then, of course, there are *techniques* and *skills*, what we sometimes call "the craft."

In visual art for instance, two-point perspective is a *technique*, a particular method of tricking the human eye into perceiving depth in a two-dimensional drawing, a technique that, once understood, can be applied to rendering all kinds of images to give the viewer the illusion of depth. In music, playing scales on an instrument is a *skill*, a neuro-muscular short-cut that, with sufficient practice and repetition, can be made semi-automatic. Flutist Jeanne Baxtresser writes:

> For the music teacher of an instrument, the first task is to simply teach the purely physiological abilities required to be able to make a beautiful sound on a piece of metal or wood. That is our fundamental work.
>
> (Baxtresser, 2010)

A great deal of arts-teaching involves instruction in such specific, teachable skills and techniques. And, as Baxtresser suggests, in some disciplines there is a great deal of technique that students must master. The question is how to teach it without killing the joy that led the student to want to study in the first place. The teacher can show a student the "proper" (usual? effective?) way in which to hold a calligraphy pen, he can explain the "right" (accepted? classic?) way of scanning "To be or not to be ... ," and he can demonstrate the "correct" (traditional? normal?) way to pass one finger over or under the others when playing a scale on the piano. But, as music educator Eloise Ristad points out, even in the realm of simple technique, things may not be so simple:

> It is scary to realize that there are many, many right ways, and that as we grow and develop, our perceptions change and shift about right or wrong ways. If we allow ourselves to become authorities, we tend to lock ourselves into the corner we label "right," and forget that every corner has its own share of rightness.
>
> The bland, innocuous C Major scale has no black keys to break up the landscape and give fingers some obvious point of reference. Thus this scale has any number of fingering possibilities that someone could decree was right.
>
> (Ristad, 1982, pp. 128, 130)

But surely some fingerings are better than others, aren't they? Perhaps. But, as Gopnik's work suggests, teaching a student the "best way" to do something may not be the best way to teach. Gopnik's study seems to imply that students learn best when they can use their brains in the freewheeling, experimental mode, a mode it once entered easily, before it was inhibited by the prefrontal cortex. But we are talking here about working with older students. What can a teacher of older students do to encourage that long-lost way of thinking?

The answer, biologist James Zull suggests, is that a teacher's first task is to reawaken a student's dormant capacity for pure discovery by encouraging pure experimentation:

> Maybe we should give students time for more random actions. Maybe we should allow them to search around for what is out there rather than insisting that their actions be focused on the task at hand. Maybe our job is to put things in their way and then stand back and let students discover them. After all, this is the biological way. It is only through exploring, through action, that we encounter new information.
>
> (Zull, 2002, p. 217)

This idea, that the teacher's job is to "put things in their way," is exactly the way Jerzy Grotowski approached teaching acting. He called this way of teaching and learning the *via negativa*:

> The education of an actor in our theatre is not a matter of teaching him something; we attempt to eliminate his organism's resistance to this psychic process. ... a **via negativa** – not a collection of skills but an eradication of blocks.
>
> (Grotowski, 1976, pp. 16–17)

VIA NEGATIVA

In the mystical Catholic tradition, a *via negativa* refers to a negative pathway to God, the acknowledgement that what is holy is ultimately unnameable. Susan Sontag writes:

> As the activity of the mystic must end in a *via negativa*, a theology of God's absence, a craving for the cloud of unknowing beyond knowledge and for the silence beyond speech, so art must tend toward anti-art, the elimination of the "subject" (the "object," the "image"), the substitution of chance for intention, and the pursuit of silence.
>
> (Sontag, 1966, pp. 4–5)

Jerzy Grotowski was fascinated with Gnostic Catholicism, its iconography, its questions, and its language. But his take on Christianity was consistently transgressive. So when Grotowski appropriated the Catholic phrase *via negativa,* he instilled it with his own meaning.

> The actor must discover those resistances and obstacles which hinder him in his creative task. Thus the exercises become a means of overcoming these personal impediments. ... By a personal adaptation of the exercises, a solution must be found for the elimination of these obstacles which vary for each individual actor. ... This is what I mean by *via negativa*: a process of elimination.
>
> (Grotowski, 1976, 1981, p. 101)

But this negative learning process can be difficult, both for students and for teachers. For students, it is not what they've come to expect from an educational experience, so it requires a very new approach to the learning process. For teachers, it can mean giving up some of the subtle gratifications we may have assumed are the best attributes of teaching. I will quickly discuss the challenges for students here. The challenge for teachers is what most of this book is about.

What students expect

Most students come to our classes after many years of what the radical Brazilian educator, Paulo Freire, refers to as "the banking concept of education":

> In the banking concept of education, knowledge is a gift bestowed by those who consider themselves knowledgeable upon those whom they consider to know nothing.
>
> (Freire, 1970, p. 53)

In the arts, the currency students expect their teachers to deposit in the learning bank is new skills. These expectations can lead students into great frustration with a teaching style that does not trade in that legal tender.

The acting classes I teach include Grotowski's *exercices plastiques*. These exercises seem at first to be simple physical isolations, lifting one shoulder, for instance, and then moving it forward and back or in circles. But the purpose of these actions lies not in the proper execution of the movements, but rather in the images and associations they provoke within the actor's mind and body. But many students, expecting that "training" means learning to properly emulate what they have been shown, immediately start to worry about whether they are doing the exercises "right." It may take them several weeks to become used to the idea that these physical isolations are not forms to be imitated or perfected. They are instead invitations to a personal investigation along the lines Gopnik talks about, permissions to engage in an inner journey, a journey of "return" to that condition in which uninhibited exploration was—and still is—possible. Ultimately, most students find that the *plastiques* do indeed provoke a condition in which images, emotions, and memories arise within them, and they discover to their delight that, with practice, they can learn to "play" the "instrument" of their bodies and imaginations as a musician might play a piano. However, because each student's tensions, inhibitions, and habits differ, *they can only discover their personal emotional "fingering" after letting go of the idea that there is a "right" way to do the exercises.* For some students letting go of that idea is the hardest part of the work.

What a student discovers in this process is not actually something "new," a skill or access to emotion he never had before; instead what he acquires is access to a skill he's always had but has learned to stifle along the way. Although these particular exercises are unique to Grotowski's work, the basic progression—applying oneself to undoing before studying new ways of doing—underlies many methods of performance training. Students studying Kristin Linklater's voice work, for instance, spend time letting go of tensions and connecting the whole body through the spine and breath before they try to produce sound. Similarly, Catherine Fitzmaurice begins her vocal training with what she calls "destructuring" before attempting "restructuring."

Music teacher Eloise Ristad tells a story that illustrates well that the most important lessons we teach are often those that allow students to recover dormant skills rather than those that inculcate new ones:

> Jack … went to great lengths explaining how difficult it was for him to play slow music. He played an adagio movement from a Beethoven piano sonata, and sure enough, he had trouble playing slow music.
>
> On the last day of the workshop, he brought in some yellowed sheet music to class. It was a set of Moravian dances, written in an improvisatory manner, full of lush romantic nuances. We were surprised when he played these with all the sensitivity and warmth that had been missing before. We were less puzzled when we learned that he had grown up in a Moravian Family, and that these dances were part of his heritage—something he felt in the marrow of his bones. He had danced to this kind of music countless times as a child, but in his adult life he had tucked away the bone feelings and the muscle memory of joyous movement. He had put a part of himself "on hold"—a part that was reluctant to be discovered and that scurried into its hole as soon as we got back to Beethoven.
>
> (Ristad, 1982, p. 7)

What this student needed was not to be taught something new, but to be aided in the process of rediscovering something old, uninhibiting an ability he'd always had. Not an additive teaching process, but a subtractive one: a *via negativa*.

So the *via negativa* is not a "doing" but a process of "undoing," of giving up the accretions of fear, doubt, and self-denigration so many of us have acquired over the years. It is a process that requires self-observation, patience, and a great deal of generosity—towards oneself. For many students, embarking upon this *via negativa* can be a wonderful surprise, for it inspires a sudden reawakening of the sort of free exploration all of us once knew. It also may lead them to:

- the discovery—or rediscovery—of memories long forgotten;
- an appreciation of the joy of living with uncertainty and doubt;
- a fascination with the very process of experimentation.

But many students also discover that this "road backwards" can be extremely uncomfortable, for it also puts them in touch with:

- anger at exercises that seem impossible to get "right," or anger at the teacher who may seem to be refusing to "teach" in the manner they expect;
- frustrations with their old habits, which have served them so well in the past but now only seem to be getting in the way, and frustrations with a process that offers no sense of completion;
- powerful inner judgments, echoes of the voices of teachers who undermined their confidence and instilled fears of inadequacy, comparison, and failure in the past;
- moments of rising fear and of feeling lost because the practices they are learning require the discovery of a forgotten kind of pleasure: the pleasure of *not* being in control.

None of these experiences—neither the pleasant nor the unpleasant—are what most students are accustomed to expect from school. It can be a steep (un)learning curve.

What teachers find

Meanwhile, teachers who wish to support their students in this adventure can encounter corresponding frustrations. Just as the students who embark upon the *via negativa* may discover that the first steps they must take are "negative" steps— giving up old ways of approaching the work, or confronting and removing blockages and judgments that inhibit free exploration—similarly, teachers who wish to support their students in this process of un-learning and self-discovery, may find that they must relinquish some of the pleasures of teaching to which they've become attached. Pleasures such as:

- the pride we take in being able to answer questions;
- the righteous indignation we experience when working with difficult students;
- the secret delight of knowing that our students are dependent upon us.

When undertaking this approach for the first time, teachers may well wonder: Does this "negative" approach to education require that we cease training our students in skills and techniques? Does this methodology leave us bereft of things to teach?

No: This approach to teaching is not a negative methodology, it is a positive attitude towards teaching and towards our students, an attitude of inquiry, of openness and naïveté. It does not demand that we abandon instructing all skills and techniques. But it does imply that, while there are many skills that our students must learn from us, there are other skills they must discover—or rediscover—on their own.[1] But which ones are which? Often enough this is something we must allow our students to teach us. Eloise Ristad describes the teaching challenge this way:

> A person must accept permission to be free of the usual restriction. Each of us is partly a childlike, unselfconscious being who can stay in the present moment without thinking of the millions of other moments in our lives. My job is not only to give a person permission to discover moment-by-moment awareness; it is to *create a climate in which that person can give herself that permission.*
>
> (Ristad, 1982, p. 6; emphasis added)

But how are we to do that? What skills must we, ourselves, learn—or un-learn—in order best to serve our students' learning and unlearning processes? That is one of the questions with which this book will grapple. And more important than the particular answers it offers, is the notion that by asking such questions of ourselves, we teachers can observe, interrogate, and revise our own teaching methods.

---

1 In *An Acrobat of the Heart* I describe several exercises that could be called "techniques": techniques for connecting the voice to the body; techniques for applying the physical work to text; and techniques for developing character work. Even then, however, each of the exercises I propose is structured as series of experiments to help the actor in making choices, rather than offering a "correct" method of speaking or moving.

Chapter 3

Questions and questioning

For the scientist the formulation of questions is almost the whole thing. The answers, when found, only lead to other questions. The nightmare of the scientist is the idea of complete knowledge.

D. W. Winnicott

During his 1967 workshop with the graduate students at New York University, Jerzy Grotowski did not permit us to take notes in class, but each evening one student went home and wrote up what he remembered of Grotowski's comments. Tom Crawley's journal, "The Stone in the Soup," records how often Grotowski insisted upon the importance of our asking questions. For instance, one day he said:

Continue searching and asking questions because answers are not fruitful, only questions are. Once you find an answer you've reached the point of stopping and must begin again.

(Crawley, 1978, p. X–2)

But when Grotowski spoke of "asking a question," he did not mean an intellectual inquiry. For him, "questioning" meant searching with one's full body for images, associations, memories, and impulses that would open us to ourselves, always looking and listening, both outside ourselves and within, for the surprises that might arise. And he made it clear that it was this act of questioning—rather than the finding of answers—that was the essential process:

having a question and not an answer to express, is why many actors are better in rehearsal than in performance. They search in rehearsal, find answers, and then perform their answers. This is not creative.

(Crawley, 1978, p. X–18)

It took me many years to understand what it was Grotowski was driving at. But little by little, I learned to perceive the ways in which the act of searching, probing, and questioning with body, voice, and image do, indeed, give rise to something special within the actor who plunges deeply into this process. Over time I got better at noticing when an actor has stopped "questioning" and has settled for an "answer." I became able to perceive the subtle change in an actor's gesture when his Romeo is no longer really reaching toward Juliet's balcony with newfound yearning but is merely repeating the gesture he discovered last week. And I began to hear the faint flatness in an actress' voice when her Juliet proclaims:

> What's Montague? it is nor hand, nor foot,
> Nor arm, nor face …

… but does so with a memorized intonation, no longer truly searching for the images, no longer quite so flustered as she adds " … nor any other part / Belonging to a man." With time, I became aware of how these slight changes could arise as responses to the enormous vulnerability that open-ended questioning demands of a performer.

The questions teachers ask

So, for a performance to remain alive, the performer must continue to ask herself questions. But in a classroom, it is often the teacher who poses the questions; and exactly how the teacher asks can make all the difference between promoting creative inquiry and shutting it down. For there are questions—and questions.

Several years ago I attended a four-day seminar called "The Artist and Model in Perspective: A Feminine View." Our teacher spoke with calm command of her subject, and on the opening day, she made it clear that one of the characteristics she considered an essential part of the "feminine view" was openness and spaciousness, the idea that truth was something that arose from process, not something imposed from above. Then, on the second day of class, as she was showing us a slide of a painting by Gustav Klimt, she turned to the class and asked, "So, what is it that is most striking in this painting?"

Rhea, a quiet young woman who had not previously spoken up in the class, raised her hand. When the teacher called on her, Rhea said that what was most striking to her in the Klimt was the fact that the woman's eyes were closed. "It's like she's asleep," she said.

The teacher, apparently disappointed with Rhea's comment, paused for a moment and then responded, "Remember what we were talking about yesterday?" She left a small pause. "What were we saying about foreground and background?" Immediately, one of the students who often participated in the discussion suggested that the human figure in the painting seemed almost to disappear within the patterns of the clothing and the background.

"Yes, exactly," the teacher nodded her head. "You might even say the woman in the picture is being 'swallowed up' by the background patterns. So, on the one hand, the artist *seems* to be venerating the model, making her beautiful, but on the other hand, what you notice—within all the gold and the glitter—is that the woman has been reduced to being a 'decorative' form. Do you see what I mean?"

Many heads nodded in agreement. I glanced over at Rhea. Rather than nodding, she seemed to be staring at the wall. What had just happened? The point our teacher had made was well taken; it seemed entirely possible that this Klimt painting did, indeed, demonstrate the thesis she was advancing, that some male artists "demean women even while praising them." And yet, and yet, as the teacher moved on to Duchamp's *Nude Descending a Staircase, no. 2*, it seemed to me that something besides the art lesson had just transpired in the classroom.

During the following days of the workshop, Rhea never spoke again. I don't know if the teacher noticed, but for me, Rhea's silence seemed to confirm a growing discomfort I experienced, for our teacher kept doing little things that rubbed me the wrong way. At the time I attributed my unease to my being a one of the few men in a feminist workshop, and to my envy of the teacher's impressive command of her subject. It was only several months later that I took the time to reexamine in my memory what it was that had bothered me the day we had contemplated the Klimt.

Like many such classroom moments, the interchange between Rhea and the teacher had passed in a couple of seconds. But in that eye-blink the teacher had accomplished two things: First of all, by not actually responding to Rhea's comment at all, she had implied that her suggestion was not worth acknowledging. Her non-reaction was, in a way, more damning than, "No, you're wrong" might have been, for that would at least have let Rhea know that she had been heard. Moreover, by saying: "Remember what we were talking about yesterday … " our teacher had altered not just the question itself but the very *nature* of the question she was asking.

Levels of questions

Educators who have studied teaching techniques say that question-asking in the classroom can be classified by the "level" of the questions being posed. The lowest level of questions is "procedural" questions, such as, "Who has his homework ready to hand in?" At the next level are questions that demand nothing more than recall of information: "When was the Battle of Waterloo?" One step above that are questions that involve reasoning, then questions that ask for opinions, and finally unanswerable, metaphysical speculations (Edwards & Bowman, 1996, p. 4). When teachers are asked about the kinds of questions they wish to be asking or to have their students asking in their classrooms, most say that they'd like to have their students thinking about the "higher level" questions rather than in merely demonstrating accurate recall. But in spite of this general—but theoretical—agreement, classroom studies indicate that this is not actually what takes place.

> Although teachers often profess to develop students' higher reasoning abilities, the types of questions they ask in class tend to require recall from memory of previously learned responses.
>
> (Edwards & Bowman, 1996, p. 5)

Or, to put it statistically:

> The findings in studies on teachers' questioning practices are fairly consistent. ... About 60% of teachers' questions require students to recall facts; about 20% require students to think; and the remaining 20% are procedural.
>
> (Gall, 1970, p. 713)

So, one way we might describe what the art teacher did while we contemplated the Klimt would be to say that when she responded to Rhea, she not only dismissed Rhea's opinion, she simultaneously "lowered" the level of the dialogue. Her original question: "What is it that is most striking in this painting?" sounded like a question of opinion, i.e. "What is most striking [to you] ... ?" But it turned out that the question she really wanted answered was not one of opinion; it was one of recall. What she wanted was for someone to remember something she had told us the previous day about foreground and background. And when she did not receive the response she was looking for, she dismissed the reply she'd received and steered the class toward the "right" answer.

Moreover she also obscured the fact that she was asking us to repeat something she herself had said. By saying "what *we were talking about* yesterday" rather than "what *I told you* yesterday" she still made it sound as though she was a member of a group which had discussed this business of foreground and background, when in fact this was a subject she had lectured to us about the previous day.[1]

Feminist psychoanalyst Gemma Fiumara points out that this sort of subtle change can have profound effects:

> The way in which a question is posed limits and conditions the quality, the level, of any answer that can possibly be worked out.
>
> (Fiumara, 1990, p. 34)

So, with a slight rhetorical twist, our art teacher had subtly imposed a limit on the level of answer that was acceptable in her class. It suddenly appeared that her questions were not to be experienced as prompts to an open-ended discussion, they were simply clues to a closed case.

Paulo Freire writes that the act of switching an open-ended question—a question of personal experience or opinion—to one of recall, is not simply a change of "level of questioning." It is, he says, an act of "violence."

> Any situation in which some individuals prevent others from engaging in the process of inquiry is one of violence. The means used are not important; to alienate human beings from their own decision-making is to change them into objects.
>
> (Freire, 1970 p. 66)

That's a pretty strong way of putting it, but if we note that after the teacher of "The Artist and Model in Perspective: A Feminine View," altered her Klimt question, Rhea never spoke up in class again, perhaps "violence" is not too strong a word.

What I found most disturbing in this art teacher's change of question, however, was that her slight-of-hand was obscured by the declared humane and progressive content of her lesson. It would be asking a lot for students of "A Feminine View" to perceive the rather patriarchal character of the instructor's teaching style. The result was that many of the students in the class actually enjoyed being treated, in Freire's terms, as "objects."

It isn't that I think the art teacher meant to silence Rhea, or even that she was aware of what she'd done. But Freire points out there is a deep

---

1 This grammatical slight-of-hand, the "royal we," was invented centuries ago by kings— and is still used today by politicians to imply, on the one hand, that the speaker is speaking *for* everyone, while it suggests at the same time that the speaker *is* everyone.

irony in trying to teach a "progressive" point of view using what he calls a "rigid" method of teaching:

> Whereas the rightist sectarian, closing himself in "his" truth, does no more than fulfill a natural role, the leftist who becomes sectarian and rigid negates his or her very nature.
>
> (Freire, 1970, p. 21)

In a less politicized vein, Anne Dalke, who teaches literature and Women's Studies at Bryn Mawr, suggests that a teacher who asks questions to which she knows the answer is not only hurting her students; she is also hurting herself:

> the advice ... I got from [my] graduate teaching instructor at Penn [was]: "Never ask a question in class if you don't know the answer."
>
> Nowadays I *only* ask a question in class if I do not know the answer. Otherwise, what's the point? I want to be in conversations going somewhere I haven't been before, teaching me something I don't know yet. If I come into class knowing what will happen, knowing everything they should know, and serve it up, where's the space for discovery?
>
> (Dalke, 2002, p. 131)

But living with questions is no easier for teachers than it is for students. Living with questions means treating each class as a "rehearsal" rather than as a "performance." When a student asks a question, it sometimes means living with the discomfort of *not* supplying the answer, even when we think we have one. That means giving up the gratification that answering gives, both to our students and to ourselves: foregoing the murmurs of appreciation students offer for an insightful comment, and the pride we take in being able to display our wisdom. And what a terrible temptation that can be.

What do teachers fear?

There are other good reasons for a teacher to slide from questions of opinion to ones of recall. Like our fear of losing control: control of the time, of the curriculum, or of our train of thought. In my own teaching I have noticed that when I fear I'm running short on time, I will start steering a discussion in the direction I want it to go. It is only later, when thinking over the class, that I will realize what I did and wonder:

What was all the hurry really about? Why did I think it was so important that I cover my curricular points? And was it really just about time?

I suspect that often, beneath my fear of not getting through the curriculum on time, lie old memories of schoolroom moments when, as a student, the classroom felt out of control in one way or another: those days when the teacher picked on me but I didn't know the answer, or the time when I was thrown into playing football without having learned the rules. These, and other moments like them, instilled in me a fear that, in one way or another, every minute of school was in some way a test that I might fail. And that antique fear runs so deeply that, every once in a while, I still have school anxiety dreams—of both kinds: student anxiety dreams that it is the end of the semester, but I haven't read the book or prepared for the upcoming test; and teacher anxiety dreams in which I'm trying to get control of my class but no one is listening. Teacher educator Parker Palmer, however, advises us to just accept our fears of school. They are there in all of us, he says, and we might as well get used to it:

> As a young teacher, I yearned for the day when I would know my craft so well, be so competent, so experienced, and so powerful, that I could walk into any classroom without feeling afraid. But now, in my late fifties, I know that day will never come. I will always have fears, but I need not be my fears—for there are other places in my inner landscape from which I can speak and act.
>
> (Palmer, 1998, p. 57)

The irony for me is that this lesson—the lesson about the necessity of accepting our fears—is a lesson I often teach my acting students. In fact, my take on fear is even more radical than Palmer's. Rather than teaching my students to find "other places ... from which ... [to] speak and act," I encourage them to accept their fear as a kind of gift, for the energy of fear can be a great wellspring of creative energy.

For instance, when I meet with a new group of students for the first time, I often begin by having them play a game of tag, not just because tag is fun—and the one game to which everyone knows the rules without needing to be taught—but also because, on the first day of class, everyone is naturally a bit nervous, and tag is a game that transforms that fear directly into creative energy. It encourages students to discover in their bodies, if not consciously, that fear—the simple fear of being tagged—is a playable emotion, a source of excitement and laughter, not something to be avoided.

Later in my curriculum, I lead students in several other fear-based exercises. I often teach the diving somersaults that Grotowski called

Tiger Leaps, an exercise that transforms fear directly into courage, and makes it clear that courage is not the same as fearlessness. Fearlessness requires a deadening of emotion, but courage faces fear and turns it into a source of creative energy. The following week, I teach my students the Just Stand exercise in which students are asked to stand, facing the audience for one minute while they "don't try to do anything." This simple exercise offers performers a dose of pure, undiluted stage fright, and it shows them how to enjoy playing even with this most universal performance problem. It is a delightful lesson of learning to enjoy what one cannot control.[2] The fact is that fear has a very bad reputation but, rightly viewed, it can prove a great source of performance energy.

I've taught these lessons over and over, so I should know them well. But when I'm teaching, the smallest moments of un-control can still unsettle me: two students whispering, or a student falling asleep, or an off-topic comment, and suddenly I fear I've lost control. Then, as I struggle to regain my balance, rather than pausing and taking stock of what just happened, I can hear myself quickly telling a lame joke or changing the subject, or simply moving on to the next curriculum point, as the Feminist art teacher did.

Better not to ask

Before we leave this issue, I want to raise one more way of looking at the moment we've been examining, the moment when the art teacher changed the nature of her question. For, looked at from another perspective, her mistake did not occur in that moment at all; it lay earlier, in her trying to ask a question when, in fact, she had no question to ask.

J. T. Dillon, one of the many educators who insist on the importance of asking questions, suggests many strategies for doing so, including "making room ... in the class agenda [for questioning], welcoming and inviting questions, and waiting patiently for them" (in Edwards & Bowman, 1996, p. 8). But Dillon also points out that there are several situations in which teachers should *not* ask questions. One of these, he says, is when you want to "elicit from a student the ... thought which has occurred to your mind." At such moments the best thing to do is simply to make "a declarative statement: express your own state of mind, your thought, your opinion, etc." (Dillon, 1981, p. 15).

In other words, the error the art teacher made did not really occur at the moment when she *switched* questions. It occurred earlier when she

---

2 Detailed descriptions of these and the other exercises I mention appear in *An Acrobat of the Heart.*

fooled us—and perhaps herself—into believing that she had a question to ask when, in fact, what she had was simply a desire to reiterate something she'd said the day before.

My point here is that, in these quicksilver moments, we teachers can mislead our classes—and ourselves—by unintentionally hiding the nature of the pedagogical transaction that is taking place, masking the fact that we are giving a lecture under the guise of having a discussion. This is exactly the kind of maneuver, educator Peter Elbow says, that teachers should try hard to avoid:

> Almost any [classroom] rules are workable so long as they are clear: "We can talk about anything so long as it has something to do with the assignment"; or, "I reserve the right to decide what the questions will be, but we can do anything in treating these questions". ... The only unworkable rule is a common unspoken one: "You must freely make my points." When I finally sensed the presence of this rule and how unworkable it was, I was forced to see that, if I feel certain points *must* be made in class, then I should make them as openly as I can—even through lectures—and not try to coax others to be my mouthpiece.
>
> (Elbow, 1986, p. 78)

If we attempt this "unworkable" strategy, the unintended message we give our students is: Do not believe what this teacher is telling you. And of course this message can undermine whatever else we may be trying to teach. To put it starkly, for Rhea and me at least, the result of the art teacher's gambit was to make us doubt *everything* the art teacher said.

Students' questions

Just as teachers can ask questions at many levels, so can students: from the procedural to the metaphysical. But for students, the very act of asking a question of any kind can be an attempt to assert control by steering the class in some direction. Therefore, for teachers, making space for questioning can "require a shift in the view of the teacher from one who acts as sole class authority to one who guides the process of teacher-student interaction—a shift that some teachers may be unable or unwilling to make" (Edwards & Bowman, 1996, p. 7). (And maybe for good reason: I remember the rather blatant attempt students would sometimes make in high school to wrest control of the class by asking the teacher irrelevant questions in the hope that she would become so caught up in answering them that she would run out of time to give us a quiz.)

It seems this subject of control keeps coming up, and we will address it directly in the chapter on Power. But for now, I'd like to examine the possibility that a student's question can also provide an opportunity to demonstrate that, as Grotowski suggested, the asking of a question might be more important than the answer.

One day my acting class had just spent 15 minutes practicing the Cat, Grotowski's full-body warm-up exercise. This exercise involves stretches, undulations, and strong kicks, and it requires a great deal of concentration and effort. It is a very invigorating workout, but the Cat can also push some students to their limits of endurance—both physical and emotional. In fact, that's part of the point, for at the limits of our endurance, we often become aware of emotions and thoughts we ordinarily avoid.

Therefore, at the end of a Cat, I often ask my students to sit in a circle and to share their experience with the group. It is a practice that immediately makes clear the enormous variety of inner experience people can have while all engaged in the same outer experience. On this particular day, most of the students in the circle said things like: "It was exciting; it made me feel sexy." Or: "My arms hurt." Or, "I kept worrying if I was doing it right." But one student said simply: "I don't understand what this has to do with acting." And then he added, "Why are we doing these exercises anyway?"

This was more than a simple question. Perhaps it expressed a serious anxiety. Perhaps it was a challenge to me. So, how should I respond? After all, the student who is issuing a challenge needs a different response from the student who is expressing his fear. So in order to figure out how to respond to such a question, we need to examine an even larger question: The question of how we listen.

Chapter 4

Listening

As a director, my biggest contribution to a production, and the only real gift I can offer to an actor, is my attention.

Anne Bogart

During my freshman year at Brandeis University, I auditioned for the Drama Department production of *Romeo and Juliet*. When the cast list was posted, I scanned the page. A freshman girl I knew was cast as Juliet, but the director, apparently unable to find an adequate Romeo at Brandeis, had cast a boy from Boston University. My roommate had been cast in the exciting part of Paris. I scanned the list several times. No mistaking it: my name was not there. I was not entirely surprised—just devastated. But two weeks later, when the actor playing Romeo's servant, Balthazar, dropped out of the production, the director offered me the part. Balthazar is a very small part even as Shakespeare wrote it, and the director had cut it even shorter. Now all that was left was one speech of five lines, so it was not surprising that the actor who had been cast in the role had quit. When the director offered me the part, I swallowed my pride and said yes.

I studied those five lines—over and over. It wasn't much, but I was going to get it right! All I had to do was listen for Romeo's line: "How fares my Juliet? that I ask again; / For nothing can be ill, if she be well," and then to respond with mine:

> Then she is well, and nothing can be ill:
> Her body sleeps in Capel's monument,
> And her immortal part with angels lives.
> I saw her laid low in her kindred's vault,
> And presently took post to tell it you.

As opening night approached, I was pretty sure I had those five lines down cold, but you can never be too sure. So, during the opening night performance, as Romeo spoke to me, I practiced my five lines a couple more times in my head ... until I became aware of a strange silence. Romeo had stopped speaking. He was just glaring at me. I had missed my one and only cue—because I hadn't been listening.

Jerzy Grotowski believed that the very core of the actor's process was not "acting," but "*reacting*." "First and foremost," he said, "there must be a physical reaction to everything that affects us" (Grotowski, 1976, p. 172). Sandy Meisner's work begins with the same assumption:

> There are two basic principles involved here. ... "Don't do anything unless something happens to make you do it. ... " [and] "What you do doesn't depend on you; it depends on the other fellow."
> (Meisner & Longwell 1987, p. 34)

On that opening night, I'd been so intent upon getting my line right that I'd failed to listen to the "other fellow" at all.

Listening to students

All performance disciplines are deeply dependent upon listening. Musicians of all kinds, dancers, and actors must all learn to "listen" aurally, visually, or kinesthetically, to many signals, often to several signals at once. So, in one way or another, all teachers of performance are also teachers of "listening."

But good teaching, which is also a kind of performance, also requires great listening, for at least two reasons: First, of course, we must listen because we are the examples our students emulate: how can we teach them to listen if we don't do it ourselves? But second, if we wish, as Eloise Ristad counsels, to "create a climate" that allows each student to "give herself ... permission," it is only by listening very carefully that we can understand exactly what sort of climate it is that each student needs.

In my acting classes, Mira was a particularly hardworking student. She entered each exercise with determination; she worked hard until the time was up, and then she would go to her notebook to write. If I gathered the group after an exercise to discuss what had happened, Mira rarely said anything; she would usually just sit there quietly, listening to others, and then, at the end of class, she'd give me a little smile and leave the room.

But one day something had changed. I'd asked the class to engage in a 15-minute *plastique river*, a physical acting exercise that encourages the actor to embody the constantly changing impulses she feels in her body and the images she perceives in her mind. It is an exercise that depends upon the actor's willingness to follow whatever arises, a kind of solo, physical jazz riff that can lead anywhere. Mira had entered the work as usual: serious and concentrated, but after about five minutes, I could see her eyes starting to wander out of the work. Occasionally her body would slump a little or stop for a moment, then she would look around, maybe stare out the window for a few seconds, and begin again. At the end of the exercise, she was in tears, huddled on the floor, holding on to her knees. I went up to her and put my hand on her back, but I could feel her pull away from my touch, so I just let her be.

After the class was over, Mira came up to me. "We need to talk," she said.

As the others left the room, I sat on the floor of the studio worrying. I didn't know what had happened, but I figured this was not going to be pleasant. I could feel my body tensing as my mind raced. Was she injured? Had I said something wrong?

Mira sat in front of me looking at the floor.

"What is it?"

"This work ... I just hate coming to this class. It's just terrifying. I have to screw up my courage every day just to walk in. I ... I don't think it should feel like this."

"I agree," I said, "I don't think it needs to feel like that."

"But it does. I hate this 'image work.' All my images are terrible. Terrible. I'm trying to do what you say. But it's all so ... depressing, or frightening, or both."

"Can you tell me what happens?"

"I just told you. Didn't you hear what I said?"

"Yes. You said the images ... "

"Don't tell me what I said. I know what I said." Mira paused for a moment, fighting back tears. "I know what I said," she repeated.

"Okay," I said, trying to be helpful, struggling to salve Mira's pain—and my own fear of having made some unperceived mistake. "Sometimes, when people find this work uncomfortable, I suggest they take some time sitting out. You could do that. Just watch for a while."

"You're ... you're ... " She breathed heavily. "You're not hearing what I'm saying."

"Okay, tell me again." I shut up. She told me again.

"No matter how hard I try, all the images I have ... are unpleasant. One after another. That's what comes up. That's what's happening."

This time I didn't say anything. We just sat there quietly for a while on the floor. Each time I thought of something to say, I thought better of it and, with some effort, forced myself to just wait. After a few minutes of silence Mira said, "What should I do?" She paused. "Is something wrong with me?"

I asked her whether she was having a similar experience in other classes.

"No, not at all. Ask Ruth, in her movement class I laugh a lot. Really, I do." Mira smiled.

"Ah," I said, "I see you're smiling now."

"I'm thinking about that class."

"Well, maybe you could just do that."

"Do what?"

"Work with that image. That's an image, you know: your memory of Ruth's class."

"Are you serious?"

"Yes ... but not 'serious.' The work doesn't have to be 'serious,' you know."

"Really?"

"Really. But you're right, it's often a problem with this acting work. People think it needs to be something 'deep,' or 'emotional,' or 'serious.' But I think what's 'serious' about acting is that it should be seriously responsive to what you need—including memories of joy." And so, after a few more minutes of discussion, Mira relaxed, having seen there was a way in which she could reenter the work. The next time we practiced *plastique rivers* in my class, she was fully engaged, and at one moment she actually laughed out loud at something her image life had evoked.

I felt relieved, and chastened. Mira had learned an interesting lesson about her seriousness, and I had learned a lesson about listening. It wasn't exactly that I hadn't been listening to Mira the first time she spoke; I had been. The problem was that I had not allowed Mira to *feel* "listened to." In my eagerness to "solve" Mira's problem, I had responded too quickly, filling up the space Mira needed *after* she spoke. Though she'd said what she had to say, she hadn't yet let go of her words, and she hadn't had time to perceive that I'd taken them in. Perhaps, I thought, listening doesn't have to stop the moment the other person ceases speaking.

Mira's learning habit was that she tried too hard. My teaching habit was similar: a feeling that I must "do" something, when all I really needed to "do" was to listen. Balthazar had returned to haunt me in a new guise.

When Sharon Baiocco and Jamie N. DeWaters studied the habits of "distinguished" and "outstanding" college teachers, trying to figure out what characteristics made them so special, what they discovered was the kind of listening we call Empathy:

> The distinguished teaching professors we observed were constantly scanning the classroom, monitoring the impact of their words and

actions on the students' faces, and observing the posture, the tone of voice and the eye contact of their students for cues of successful communication. ... Empathy is the outer-directed equivalent of self-awareness.

(Baiocco & DeWaters, 1998, p. 121)

What makes empathy hard is that it is an act of reception, of listening, not something one can "do" at all. Like the "undoing" of the *via negativa,* this kind of "not doing" is not easy.

Listening to space

Psychologist Daniel Goleman points out that "listening" is not just something one does with one's ears:

One rule of thumb used in communications research is that 90 percent or more of an emotional message is nonverbal. And such messages— anxiety in someone's tone of voice, irritation in the quickness of a gesture—are almost always taken in unconsciously, without paying specific attention to the nature of the message, but simply tacitly receiving it and responding.

(Goleman, 1995, pp. 97–98)

In fact, it can be very helpful to begin "listening" not with one's ears but with one's body because our bodies naturally know how to "listen" on an emotional level—not just to gestures, but to space itself. In my first class with a new group of actors, I usually ask the students to explore the studio, to feel how the space affects them, to sense where they feel safe in the space and where they feel vulnerable. As they explore the space, some students will gravitate to the corners of the room, some will seek the light, some will climb on top of the furniture while others hide underneath it. The exercise makes our innate ability to "listen" to space quite clear and palpable. On the following days, I often encourage students to continue to refine their abilities in listening to the space: Where do you want to sit today? How is the light from the window affecting you? Where do you want to be in relationship to the teacher? And what happens to you if you purposefully make a choice to change where you are? I point out to my students that, as they become aware of their physical reactions to the space they are not just improving their spatial awareness, they are also attuning themselves to the existence of the many subtle signals that their bodies can sense if they allow themselves to "listen"—signals that will serve their acting in many ways.

Similarly, as a teacher, when I enter the studio, I always take a minute to listen to the space and to adjust. What kind of relationship to the space do I need today, for myself and for today's lesson? Do I need to rearrange the furniture or adjust the lights or the heat or clean the floor before we begin? Then, I often wander through the space myself, sensing where I would feel most comfortable today in relation to the class.

I know that wherever I choose to sit, my presence there will affect the students. When they spread out in the studio to do their personal warm-ups, their awareness of my being at one side of the room will often result in there being fewer students warming up on my side than on the other side. So to help the students notice how their spatial relationship to the teacher is affecting them, I will move myself to different places while they work. Immediately they will sense how the space has changed because the teacher is now in a different place, and so they will learn something about how they are "seeing" the teacher.

Later, when they join me in a circle to talk, there will often be some students who tend to sit near the teacher and others who will always sit across the circle from me. In some classes, there are students who always sit slightly behind the line of the circle. Each of these spatial choices contains information. When I call the class together, the very size of the circle tells me a lot: Almost always, after the class has participated in an intense group exercise, the circle will be tighter than it was before the exercise because the students now feel greater safety with each other. If, on the other hand, the circle has grown larger, I will suspect that something is going on; perhaps there is an unspoken issue this class needs to discuss.

Listening to bodies

When Jerzy Grotowski would comment on our work, he seemed to have an uncanny ability to "read" an actor's body. At the time, it seemed to me some sort of magic. Later, when I watched my friend Linda Putnam teaching, I saw the same thing. She would say to an actor, "There, now, it's in your upper back. Try arching a little." And I'd wonder how she knew. It took me several years, but over time, I became aware that as I watched actors working, I could actually sense the students' blockages within my own body. As they performed a scene or a monologue, I could feel my own back hunching, a tensing in my arms, a pushing or a reaching. Sometimes I would have a subliminal sense that my body wanted to collapse, to turn, or to scream. And over time I began to trust that these sensations I felt in my own body could provide the information I needed to help a student who was running into a performance problem.

When an actor's arms or his lower-body suddenly drop out of the work, it feels to me as if my own body has suddenly hesitated, as if my own arms or legs or pelvis have frozen. When I hear the actor's voice go to a whisper because he is holding back his anger, I feel as if I myself want to scream. (Sometimes at such moments, if I think the actor can work with it, I'll actually let myself call out, "the arms" or "the whisper." At other times I will just note what my body is telling me and try, after the scene is done, to help the actor remember what happened and discover the blockage for himself.) It feels to me as if this kind of listening is like the listening I do when I dance, when my body is moved directly by the music, without any interference from my mind.

During an open group warm-up, if, while I watch an actor work, my body senses some sort of a blockage, I will sometimes just join the work myself and let my body "talk" directly to the student's body. For instance, with an actor whose lower body keeps dropping out of the work, I might just put my back against his back, or place my feet against his feet and push. As soon my legs are pushing hard, his will be also. I've "heard" what his body was saying, and he's experienced a new way of working with his lower body, all without a word being said.

In the 1930s, psychoanalyst D. W. Winnicott noticed a similar phenomenon when observing mothers with their infant children. What he saw was that each mother would automatically mirror her baby's emotions, altering her own face expression to reflect what she saw in the baby's face. Winnicott theorized that by doing so, the mother was "giving back to the baby the baby's own self" (Winnicott, 1967, p. 118). He described this act of mirroring as an essential parenting reflex, a kind of physical echo that actually helps the infant experience his own emotions for the first time.

Winnicott's formulation makes it clear that, in order to "teach" the infant, the mother must simultaneously be learning *from* him. A couple of years ago, when a student returned with her newborn to visit the Naropa University MFA Theater: Contemporary Performance from which she had graduated the year before, I asked her, "How is it going with the baby?"

"We're learning the ropes," she said. And indeed this "learning" is a two-way activity. While the child is learning to experience itself through the mother's expressions, the mother is "learning" to distinguish all the signals: the difference between the cries of hunger, the screams of pain, and the whines of tiredness. Similarly, a teacher who listens to her students with her whole being becomes able to be helpful through "learning" what the student is experiencing. In this process, the teacher is not just an observer, but also a vicarious participant, for the sensation the student feels is mirrored within the teacher's body and brain. Recently neurologists, using brain-imaging techniques, have monitored the role of "mirror neurons," brain cells that fire when observing another person's movements or emotion.

MIRROR NEURONS

A group of Italian neuroscientists noticed that identical nerve cells discharge both when a monkey performs a specific action and when it observes another monkey performing that action. The researchers dubbed these newly discovered neurons mirror neurons because of the way they apparently mirrored an observed action in the monkey's brain. A monkey grabs a peanut and the monkey watching activates the same synaptic pathways. But actually, both monkeys are doing. One monkey is visibly making an action; the other monkey is restraining from making the exact same action.

It turns out that humans have mirror neurons too. The observation of a goal-oriented action triggers the identical synaptic activity in the observer as in the person who is generating the action. The act of watching is not psychological interpretation or conjecture; rather the act of watching is physical and energetic. Attentive watching charges our bodies with electric currents. The mirror neuron activity creates a simulation of the activity being observed in the observer's brain and in this way the observer seems to gain a deeper understanding of a particular movement through actual physical simulation and stimulation.

Mirror neurons are the cells that relate to empathy. Via action, mirror neurons create a meaningful link between the self and the other by dissolving the boundary between the two. When mirror neurons are activated, people feel empathy (Bogart, 2010).

Listening to what is—and is not—said

When a warm-up or a scene presentation is over, I usually ask my students to take a minute to sense what they are feeling, and to remember what they have experienced. Then I begin the feedback by asking the actors to talk about their own experience in the work. (More on this in the chapter on Feedback.) As they do, I find there is often as much information in *how* they speak, and in what they do *not* say, as there is in the words they do say.

Two actors had just finished showing a section of the scene in John Patrick Shanley's play *The Dreamer Examines his Pillow* in which Tommy confesses that he has had sex with Donna's sister. At the climax of the scene the two characters get into a big verbal fight which ends with a kiss:

TOMMY: You still love me.

DONNA: Yeah, I love ya. I dote on ya. I hate your fuckin guts. I'm lost how to proceed with you. You're like a nut. You see everything through this slot. It kills me. I thought you loved me.

TOMMY: I do.

DONNA: I don't get it. How could you love me and drag my family down into this shit?

TOMMY: Why do you think I'm sittin in this garbage can? Huh? Cause everything's cool an I'm in good shape? Huh? Look at me. Look at my picture I did. That's me. One eye sees too much one eye can't get big enough to see my way out of how I feel, I'm holdin my face up with nails. Everything's you. I see everything and everything's you. *He grabs her and crushes her. They kiss passionately.*

(Shanley, 1992, p. 83)

The scene started out well enough, but as it progressed, the two actors seemed more and more uncomfortable, and by the time they reached the climax, their bodies were almost motionless. After they had finished, when the two of them spoke to the class about their work, the woman said she'd had real difficulties speaking Shanley's New York slang, the man said he knew he wasn't always taking in what she was saying, and both of them agreed that they needed to get much more precise with what they were doing—but neither of them mentioned the fact that they had entirely avoided the fight and the kiss that the scene called for.

After they'd spoken, I said, "I'm just wondering, did you two ever touch each other during a rehearsal?"

They both looked down at the floor. "Yeah," the man said. "One night we really got into the fight ... "

"And how was that?"

A pause.

The woman said, "Well we realized we needed to choreograph the fight. And ... "

"And ... ?"

After another pause, the man answered. "And then we kinda lost track of the rehearsal."

So I talked about the importance of choreographing violence—and sex—and suggested that at their next rehearsal they figure out how to deal with both of those energies very technically. By working very slowly, and by constantly checking in with each other, they would be able to monitor all the fears and excitements a punch or a kiss can evoke, and make whatever adjustments their safety and their creative intuitions required. By *not* mentioning the problems the violence and the intimacy of the scene had presented, they had made it plain how very difficult and how important those questions were.

The ocean of questioning

At other times, as I listen, what I may perceive is a disconnection between what the actor's words are saying and what his body is telling me. A few years ago I was working with a young actor named Samuel on the speech from *Richard II* in which the King bitterly accedes to Bolingbroke's demand that he surrender and descend from the ramparts of his castle. The whole way through the speech, Samuel had held his hands tightly in front of him. When he was done, I asked him whether he'd been aware that he'd done that, and he had a ready answer: "Oh, yes. That's because Richard is on the balcony and holding on to the balustrade." It seemed clear to me that Samuel was uncomfortable in his body and that his insecurity was showing itself in his literally "holding on." But his quick answer also alerted me to the fact that he was equally uncomfortable with the kind of body-centered acting language I often use. I felt pretty sure that his gesture of "holding on to the balustrade" served Samuel as a way to stay in control of himself during the scene, but listening to his response, it was also plain to me that it would not be helpful for me to offer my opinion about this gesture. He had his answer, and it was important to him to have an answer. Being uncertain of anything was very difficult for him.

So, searching for an approach that would play to Samuel's strength, I asked him to talk about the historical circumstances behind this dramatic moment. Suddenly he was animated. He lit into a fascinating lecture on late Medieval English history. He told us about how Richard's father, the Black Prince, had died before he could inherit the throne, how Richard had seized the land of the five "lords appellant," and about how Bolingbroke had rallied his forces while Richard was off pursuing more conquests in Ireland. As Samuel regaled us with this history, his body relaxed and his arms gesticulated wildly.

"Keep going," I coached, "that's great. Just look down at Bolingbroke as you do." Sam now aimed his history lecture toward the imaginary usurper. "Good," I said, "now just pick up the monologue, anywhere."

Samuel was fully animated now, and he had forgotten all about the balustrade. He barreled through the whole speech with great energy—and with no holding on. Two days later Samuel came up to me in the hallway. "I'm sorry about two days ago. I know I was being difficult. I guess you were right about the balustrade. I didn't really need it. I don't know why I thought I did."

This admission marked a turning point in our relationship. It was not that Samuel suddenly gave up his stiffness or his intellectual approach to text, but his "I don't know why … " was the first time he'd admitted—to me, and perhaps to himself—that he had new things to learn in this class. It was a sign that he was actually accepting me as a teacher, and an indication that he could allow himself to swim in the ocean of questioning, rather than holding on to the dry land of ready answers.

Listening between the lines

Another situation in which I find myself listening-between-the-lines is when I'm helping students choose their acting scenes. Having watched a group for several weeks of training exercises leading up to the scene-work, I often have a pretty good idea of what kind of scene might serve each one. But even so, I always start the scene-selection process by asking them for their ideas. Often enough they will choose scenes that, for one reason or another, won't work very well as training tools, and then I'll have to offer them other choices. But even when their selections must be rejected, I have learned a lot from seeing which scenes they'd pick for themselves. If they suggest love scenes, or violent ones, or homosexual scenes, they've given me information that will help me understand how they experience themselves. And if they select characters who do or don't match their own ethnicity or race, they provide a glimpse of the range of characters they feel comfortable portraying. Often this is information the students are not ready to say in so many words. Sometimes it is information they don't even know they know about themselves.

And then there are those times when I can learn something valuable by listening to something I was *not* supposed to hear. Here's an example occasioned by another Cat. The day before, my class had studied the Cat exercise long and hard. Aware that there might be some resistance, I announced that today we were going to try the same exercise again. As I spoke, from somewhere in the circle I heard a slight groan … very slight. I was pretty sure I knew where the groan had come from; the young woman with the long black hair who'd been staring at the floor all morning. I couldn't be sure, but it was clear that someone in the circle really didn't want to do another Cat.

I could have just ignored the sound and continued to set up the exercise without comment. Or I could have gone the other way and said, "Ah, did someone groan?" But I wanted to find a way to acknowledge the groan without pointing a finger. So, at the end of our discussion I said, "Now we'll begin our Cats, but let's do this: If you want to do the Cat now, go ahead. If you want to just watch and take notes, that's okay too. You decide. But if you do choose to do another Cat, remember that this form is meant to serve the material—your material. Your job is to allow whatever you are feeling right at the moment to affect how you do the exercise. For instance, if you were feeling like it's a struggle just to get yourself to do the exercise at all, the question is: how can you allow that struggle inform your Cat? Maybe you take longer just to begin. Maybe your Cat keeps changing its mind, stopping, quitting, and starting again. But as you work, keep checking in with yourself because your feelings may change. You may be surprised. Okay. We're starting now. I'll tell you when there are three minutes left."

I still don't know for sure it was she who groaned, but the girl with the long black hair did an amazing Cat that day. It was filled with sudden starts and stops, moments of complete collapse, and flashes of anger; and as she worked, she sometimes glared at me and at one point broke into derisive laughter. When the group gathered at the end of the exercise to share, she didn't have anything to say, but she was no longer staring at the floor.

Unspoken questions

So now, while we're observing Cats, let's return to the situation that inspired this chapter in the first place: What to say to the student who said, "I don't understand what this has to do with acting. Why are we doing these exercises anyway?"

The first thing to note is that this kind of question may require some forbearance; if I take it as a personal attack, I'll only get myself in trouble. (More on this in the chapter on Transference.) Instead, my response to this kind of question is often more of a response to the student than it is an answer to the question itself, for I am not just listening to the words but to the student's tone of voice and his body-language. I am trying to understand why is he asking this particular question at this moment. Is it an expression of his frustration with the Cat we just completed? Is he asking for personal reassurance that he's doing okay, or is his question his way of letting me know he's angry with me? Or is it perhaps that, like Samuel, he is a person who needs to grasp things with his mind before he feels safe taking risks with his body?

Beyond that, I'll also be taking into account how the other students are reacting to this question. Are they nodding their heads, indicating that the whole group needs some kind of explanation before we go further, or does another student quickly try to answer the first one? And if so, does the second student's answer leave the first student in need of some support, some indication from me that I am not offended by his having asked the question?

If I sense that the question is inspired by the fact that the Cat has actually had a strong effect upon the questioner, I might say simply: "That's a good question. I wonder if you can live with that question for a while without needing to have an answer." If I've guessed right, the student will take my non-answer as a useful challenge or as permission to allow his discomfort with the work to be an energy source for future exercises. And if I've guessed wrong ... Well, let's come back to those cases later.

However, if, in the student's "Why are we doing these exercises anyway?" I hear a plaintive appeal for succor, it can be difficult not to just say: "Well, actually, the reason we are doing this exercise is because it will connect your body with your inner emotional life." That *is*, of course, a central reason we are doing this exercise, but to give this kind of response might distract the student from the tentative steps he is taking down his personal *via negativa*. For in spite of the fact that the student is finding the work frustrating—or rather *because* he is—his question implies that the exercise is actually doing what it is designed to do: start him on his way down the road by awakening in him an awareness of the emotions he is experiencing. So my response must be aimed at encouraging his act of questioning.

"You're asking the right question," I might say. "Maybe you can try this: The next time you do a Cat, perhaps in tomorrow's warm-up, you might look for a Cat who lives with just such questions. What happens to your Cat if he is plagued by doubt?"

At such moments, what's hardest for me is if I sense that a student is asking his question out of real trepidation: the fear that he can't trust this new teacher, the fear that he's in the wrong class, the fear that he shouldn't be studying acting at all. When I sense that, then *that* is the issue I will try to address. The student who is looking for some reassurance needs to feel that I hear him. That's why it is important that I begin with, "That's a good question." And then perhaps I'll say, "That is actually a question we asked Grotowski when he taught us this work in 1967, because working this way seemed so strange to us. And it took us quite a while to understand that when Grotowski said the value of these exercises 'lies in our *not* being able to do them' he was not just trying to sound mysterious. He really meant that our frustration, and especially our awareness of our frustration, was not a bad thing, but a good one."

Even as I try to speak to this student's fears, I must avoid the temptation to simply assuage his discomfort, for it is also important for him to see that, although feeling such fear and frustration may worry *him*, it doesn't trouble me. Even if *he* is worried the water is too deep, *I* perceive that he can swim.

The truth is, this student's question *is* a good question, a question that needs asking, but that does not mean it is one that calls for an answer. By answering it too entirely, I might salve his exasperation—and mine—but only at the risk of prolonging his process of discovery.

So, the question of how we listen inevitably leads into the question of how we respond, how we give feedback. The problem is: no matter how well we have listened, when we respond, each student will hear our comments through the filter of his own judgments and his expectations about what feedback and criticism are or should be.

Chapter 5

Feedback

> Whenever you have truth it must be given with love, or the message and the messenger will be rejected.
>
> Mahatma Gandhi

At the beginning of Stanislavski's book, *Building a Character*, the young actor Kostya is struggling with his acting. He's floundering around, not knowing how to begin. Then one day, in desperation, he uncovers a character within himself, a character whom he calls "the Critic." This personage, whom he builds with costume, makeup, and physical choices, describes himself as: "The fault-finding critic who lives inside of Kostya Nazvanov. I live in him in order to interfere with his work. That is my great joy. That is the purpose of my existence" (Stanislavski, 1949, p. 15).

Kostya's internal Critic is a type of character we all carry in our heads. By the time we're teenagers most of us are well acquainted with the internal voices that tell us what's wrong with our bodies, looks, habits, prospects for happiness, and with our performances.

I, for instance, remember quite well the day I learned how *not* to sing. It was in fifth-grade chorus class, and the group was singing some song in two-part harmony. At one point, the teacher stopped us and asked us all to repeat one phrase. As we sang, he scanned the group, listening intently. At the end of the phrase, he pointed at me and said simply, "You ... don't sing." Then he raised his hands for the group to start the song again. As the other kids around me sang, I silently moved my lips. Ever since, I've felt very insecure when trying to sing.

Infants are born without vocal insecurities. But along the road to adulthood, as we learned to sit still in our seats and raise our hands, most of us have also learned—in one way or another—to Be Quiet! Young women often learn to keep their voices in the upper register while men learn the opposite and try to avoid the head-voice altogether. Many actors, of both sexes, just as the scene they are playing becomes most dramatic, suddenly start to whisper their lines. As I suggested in the chapter on the *via negativa*, what these actors need is not the learning of a brand new skill. What they need is to "unlearn" an inhibition of a skill they've always had.

Teaching this lesson can be a very delicate task, for the negative voices that reverberate in our minds were once learned for very good, self-protective reasons. In our world, the power of these nagging, negative voices—the internalized echoes of prohibitions imposed by our parents and our teachers, voices that Augusto Boal called "the cop in the head"—has been reinforced by the advertising-saturated environment in which we live, a world which inundates us with images of others who are stronger, slimmer, cooler, richer, and happier than us because they have better skin, faster gadgets, and newer wardrobes. Madison Avenue discovered long ago that advertising is most effective when it makes us feel inadequate.

Several years ago, I directed an interview-based play about advertising and addictions. As one psychologist we interviewed for that show succinctly put it:

> Advertising is designed to generate endless self-criticism, to generate all sorts of doubts and then to offer the entire world of consumer goods as salvation. In contrast, the one message you will never hear in advertising is, "You're okay. You don't need anything. Just be you."
>
> (McGrane, 1998)

Inundated daily by such messages, it is not strange that most of us have deeply ingrained doubts about ourselves.

In common parlance, the word "critical" has come to mean simply, "bad." As in: "Most reviews of his work have been extremely *critical*." Or even worse: "He entered the hospital in *critical* condition." So when students ask for "criticism" what they often mean is "point out to me what's wrong with my work." It is almost as if they were hungering for an old, accustomed sting, in the same way a body-builder, having once heard the shibboleth, "No pain, no gain," might drive himself each day towards the muscle-burn, until, in Pavlovian fashion, he has forgotten about the gain and has become addicted to the pain.[1] Eloise Ristad says

---

1 Studies have shown that after reading a "women's magazine" women feel more depressed than before they opened the magazine. And yet these magazines sell well—very well. See Jeanne Kilbourne (1999) *Can't Buy My Love: How advertising changes the way we think and feel*, Touchstone, Simon and Schuster, NY, p. 133.

she was shocked when she first realized that music students had acquired this sort of edu-masochism:

> David Burge, now head of the piano department at Eastman School of Music, Rochester, N.Y., first pointed out to me the possibility of addiction to humiliation when I was voicing indignation over the authoritarian "teach by humiliation" style of a number of teachers at a summer music festival. "It's addictive, Eloise," I remember him saying. "Students hate it, but always assume they deserve it, and keep going back week after week for more." Frightening.
>
> (Ristad, 1982, p. 197)

Thoroughly entrained by so many "critical" voices, most American students enter each class and face every teacher with the expectation— perhaps even the desire—that the teacher will tell them what is *wrong* with what they are doing. That situation can be a real trap for teachers, for whatever we say, our words may be viewed through this dark lens. If we say something positive, our words can be dismissed, and if we say something negative, our words can be taken as confirmation of the student's general opinion that she's not doing very well.

The problem is that, even when we teachers are aware of these dangers, we can become seduced into encouraging this attitude among our students, because it builds up our own sense of self-worth. Eloise Ristad describes how she herself fell into such a trap with one of her clarinet students:

> If one of my suggestions didn't work, she took it as tangible proof of her own incompetence and lack of talent. When something *was* effective, she gave all the credit to me. It was great for my ego, and it was great for her clarinet playing—temporarily. But sooner or later she needed to start discovering her own authority rather than being convinced of my authority.
>
> (Ristad, 1982, p. 198)

So what should one do? Maybe it's better to say nothing at all?

But, of course that won't help. Most students expect feedback from their teachers; they yearn for it so strongly that it is virtually impossible *not* to give feedback. If we remain silent, our students will just read our reticence as negative feedback anyway. Our smiles, our glances, and our posture: they're all feedback to a student who is hungry for teacherly guidance. I certainly remember how desperately I myself hung on Grotowski's every word when he spoke about my work. I listened as full of fear and hope as an accused man listens to the verdict from the judge. For feedback is power-filled. And, for better or worse, a teacher must say something. The question is: Is there a way to say something that simultaneously speaks to the particular moment (e.g., the piece the student has just performed) while promoting the student's slowly developing ability to give himself the feedback he needs? Or, to put it another way: *How is one to teach without reinforcing a student's dependence upon being taught?*

As the chapter on Questions suggested, one approach to this conundrum is to get into the habit of posing questions that *really are* questions. As I've said, after an exercise like the Cat, I usually ask people to describe their experience of the exercise. Then, to emphasize the fact that there is no "right" answer to this question, I make a point of saying "Good," to all kinds of response. After a few such feedback rounds, students get the idea that in this class they can say absolutely anything.

Similarly, when I start a Shakespeare class, I almost always ask students to describe their past experiences with Shakespeare's plays. Of course there are many who say they have loved Shakespeare since they first ran across him; but often there are a few whose most salient memories are of having been forced to attend boring productions in grade school or being subjected to recitations of incomprehensible soliloquies by pompous English teachers. I'm always grateful when those students speak up, for their open disgust with The Bard makes it plain that, in our class, opinion is not something one is expected to inculcate from the teacher. The result is that when they start presenting work in class, they know that when I ask, "How did that go for you?" it is not a trick question to which I have the correct answer.

But what about giving actual feedback? Well, perhaps it is time I try to articulate an answer to the student I described in the Preface, the woman who expressed surprise when, after each monologue, I insisted that an actor give herself positive feedback; the young teacher who initiated the writing of this book by asking me, "Why do you do that?"

Seeing oneself

In the chapter on the *via negativa*, I suggested that for students to undo the blocks that inhibit their creativity, they must let go of their notion that "learning" always means acquiring new skills from a teacher. (It is a paradoxical truth that it is up to the teacher to "teach" that lesson.) So, an essential part of giving feedback is helping students understand that they may not really *need* feedback—or rather that, bit by bit, they can discover how to get the feedback they need from another source within themselves.

So, before we tackle the question of whether the feedback is positive or negative, there are at least two good reasons to begin any feedback session by asking a student first to give feedback to himself. First of all, as I pointed out in the chapter on Listening, what the student says about his own work provides a context. By asking the student to speak first, I put myself in the position of listening to the workings of his mind. Is he thinking technically, about things like the rhythms, the gestures, or the blocking, or is he more concerned with the emotion he's experiencing—or not experiencing—during the scene? The language he uses will help me find the kind of words he can hear. As I said in the story of Samuel, the actor who held on to the balustrade, what's the point of my saying something—even something wise—if he's unable to take it in?

Second, I am always concerned with the "meta-lesson" about how students can become their own teachers, so I see each and every training exercise and scene-sharing as an opportunity for them to improve their ability to perceive their work while it is happening. If I offer my opinion before students have time to voice their own, my words may carry such authority that they can erase any nascent insights that a student is beginning to have into his own processes.

Actress and teacher Uta Hagen wrote:

> Another aspect of freeing the students from overreliance on the teacher is to develop the *self-evaluation* of their work. I always ask them for it immediately after a presentation of a scene or exercise and *before* I have offered my own criticism. Self-evaluation is an important part of the actor's growth in any event. Since neither teacher nor director is likely to be present at the performances following an opening night, the actors will cease to improve in their parts unless they themselves have learned to recognize their flaws and how to correct them.
>
> (Hagen, 1991, p. 292)

When I first ask a student, "How did that go?" she will often respond, "I don't remember," insisting that she can't recall at all how the scene she just finished went. What remains in her mind seems to her a blur, like the feeling left over from a dream. But with a little probing, with a few reminders of actions or particular lines, the details will appear and the performance amnesia will be lifted.

Actress Erica Fae suggests that each performer contains an "observer," a part of her mind that can perceive and remember what she is doing while she works. With practice, the performer will discover that she can recall a great deal of detail, which means that she has, in fact, been noticing what happens even as it happens.

Such a self-awareness is not the same as "self-consciousness"—the uncomfortable sensation I used to feel on stage as a young actor when I thought, "I don't know what to do with my hands." Rather than an out-of-body feeling of self-consciousness, the self-awareness that Fae is talking about here is very much a feeling of being *in* one's body. The experience is a paradoxical one: the performer feels at once fully engaged— perhaps almost "consumed" by the energy, the emotion, the movement and music of the moment—and yet, at the same time, he finds he can witness what he is doing. When performers are "in the zone" like this, they sometimes feel as though time has slowed down. They find they have no problem making tiny "mid-course" corrections and adjustments, altering the smallest details of an arpeggio or the exact placement of the voice, reacting to the other performers or to the audience—all without missing a beat.

To help actors develop the ability to notice such minute physical, vocal, and emotional choices as they flit by, I often encourage them at first to practice rehearsing very short sections of text. Once they become aware of this ability, they can soon observe longer and longer sections, so that, by the second or third time a student presents a scene in my class, she is usually able to describe a great deal of what happened during her run-through.

Nonetheless, I have found that if I simply suggest at the end of a scene or monologue presentation that a student give herself feedback, she is very likely to begin by voicing the words of the Critic in her head, sounding notes that are often harsh and rarely helpful. Even if she is able to recall specific moments of her performance, the particulars they articulate may be a litany of what went wrong:

"Oh, I don't know. I kept going up on my lines, and in that middle section I forgot what I'd planned to do. ... It went so much better yesterday in rehearsal." Negative, and vague at the same time!

That is why, after years of experimentation, I have found it most helpful to actually insist that an actor begin with the (sometimes quite difficult) task of articulating her own positive feedback.

The secure partner

Jerzy Grotowski pointed out that, "The work of the actor is in danger; it is submitted to continuous supervision and observation" (Grotowski, 1976, p. 179). In order to withstand that situation, he urged actors to discover within themselves the diametric opposite to Kostya's Critic: not just an "observer" but a *supportive* observer; "the 'secure partner,' this special being in front of whom he does everything, in front of whom he plays with the other characters and to whom he reveals his most personal problems and experiences" (p. 203). It is not that the performer must free himself of all his inner critics—that's an impossible task—but rather that each performer can nurture this supportive inner critic, the kind and wise inner eye in front of whom he can feel safe, unguarded and open. If, as Baiocco and DeWaters say, "empathy is the outer-directed equivalent of self-awareness," this "secure partner" could be thought of as a kind of self-directed empathy, the capacity to witness the details of one's work with a benevolent precision. Grotowski believed that each of us contains this positive critic, but that his voice has been drowned out by the cacophony of negative voices we've learned to attend to. *I believe that the teacher's most essential job is to help the student hear this voice*. But often that is not an easy thing to do.

So nowadays I'll often start the feedback by saying, "Think about how your scene went, and then begin by telling us about three moments that worked well for you." For even in the worst run-throughs, some small moments, some gestures, some line-readings, some timings went well, or at least better than others. The problem is that many students tend to dismiss *all* the good work, or to take it for granted, as if it carried no weight—compared to the valuable lessons they believe they can learn from their mistakes. As one of Eloise Ristad's music students put it:

> My good performances are *always* accidents. ... I guess I feel that way about a lot of stuff in my life. ... I sort of shrug off my successes but get preoccupied with possible failures.
>
> (Ristad, 1982, p. 45)

When I insist on their beginning with the positive, some students—well schooled in negative criticism—will bristle at the idea of naming what went well. They fear it's just a wussy, New Age cop out. So I have to explain, "No, I'm not encouraging you to become a Pollyanna. It's not that your self-evaluation should exclude what went wrong. But if you *begin* with the downbeat criticisms, those gloomy comments can so cloud the atmosphere that the more affirmative ones may become completely obscured. Positive feedback is rather like dreamwork: If you don't try to remember your dream the moment you wake up, it can slip away from you entirely. Similarly, if you don't name the things that went right in your run-through immediately, they can be much harder to recapture later." Then I add, "Don't worry, your negative self-criticisms have terrific staying power. They'll still be quite plain to you after you're done with the positive ones."

But even with this encouragement, a surprising number of students will still struggle when trying to accomplish this task. Often, as a student attempts to list "three moments that worked," she will quickly insert a "but":

"I guess one moment in the scene that worked for me was when I was angry with Mary [her scene partner], and I picked up the broom to begin sweeping the room, but then I realized that it might have been better if I'd swept for a moment, and then thrown the broom on the floor, and ... "

"I understand," I interrupt to point out that the actor has slyly amended her report of "moment that worked" to include her thoughts about what didn't work. "It is true," I say, "that there is always more you can do, and when you go back to work on that moment next time, you'll probably want to experiment with how to make that sweeping moment even better. But right now you're not working on the scene. You're just giving yourself some feedback on the version you just presented, and I'm urging you to just experience what it feels like to describe a moment that worked for you, with no qualifications, and then to put a period to the sentence. By simply, technically, stopping the sentence there, you can find yourself in the uncomfortable position of having to come face to face with a smidgeon of pure satisfaction. Which, it seems to me, might serve you well."

When I say this, the student looks at me with a mixture of a smile and consternation, so I add, "Is that hard?"

"Yes," she admits, smiling again.

"Well," I say, "That's the thing about this work. It's not easy. But what makes it hard is often not what we think of as 'hard work.' What makes it hard is the discovery that the muscles that need the most work are not the pectorals or the quads. The muscles that need the most work are the small ones, like the facial muscles that allow one to smile at one's own work."

She's shaking her head, so I add, "Of course, I know that for many of us that can be very hard. Giving oneself even one unqualified compliment can be really painful. You may have to begin by taking small steps in that direction. So, how about this: The next time you come to the place in the sentence where your mind starts to insert the word 'but,' try simply inserting an 'and' instead: 'I really liked the way it felt when I started sweeping the floor. *And* the next time I do the scene, I'm going to hit the wall with the broom.' It's a small thing, but the word 'but' can undermine and undo all the positive feedback you've given yourself in the first half of the sentence, while the word 'and' helps you notice that you've actually got two, separable thoughts there: One about what worked, and a second one about what more you could do." (Another way of thinking about this problem is that the word "but" contains within it the hidden hope that things could have—or should have—been different. It carries within it a sense of regret that keeps the fantasy of an alternative past alive. "And," on the other hand, separates out what happened in the past from what more can be done in the future.)

It took this student several weeks of practice, but slowly she got the hang of putting a full stop at the end of a positive thought, although occasionally, after making some new, insightful observation about her own work, she would add, plaintively, "But what did *you* think?"

"Do you really want to know?"

"Yes."

"Well, it's just my opinion you understand, but I think the scene has come a long way. For instance, that moment with the broom. Now you know exactly on which word of the text to pick up the broom, and when to stop sweeping. Am I right?"

"Yes, it's true. But it's helpful hearing it from you."

Behind this story lies a difficult truth: The ability to give oneself helpful feedback signals a real loss, the loss of dependency upon the teacher. It is a feeling that "If I can give myself the feedback I need, maybe my teacher won't feel that he needs to give it to me anymore." This independence can take a great deal of strength, and at first, it can feel awfully lonesome.

Of course, this process can be a difficult one for teachers too because, as Mary Rose O'Reilley relates, it often goes against our own experience and expectations:

> Recently I was talking about the use of positive reinforcement in the classroom with an unusually gentle young education major who had quite a lot of teaching experience. Even this kindly, well-disposed young man had to say, "I find it difficult to give my students the affirmation they need. I didn't get it myself as a student. You have to unlearn as a teacher more than you learn."
>
> (O'Reilley, 1993, p. 31)

Another reason to encourage positive criticism is that, even when negative criticism is very perspicacious, it can leave the student with nothing to work on. Negative criticism is useful only when it is linked to a suggestion about how to improve the situation, or at least some encouragement in that direction. Without that, working with negative criticism is like not thinking about an elephant. It leaves the student with nothing to concentrate on but worrying about what *not* to do.

Later on, out in the "real" world, students are going to face all kinds of "criticism," sometimes from newspaper writers or others who think of criticism as a blood sport. Some artists survive these killing fields by developing a thick, pachidermic skin, a toughness that can wall them off from experiencing the cruelty of nasty critics. But they do so at the risk of also walling themselves off from the wide range of tender emotions their art-making requires. How much more powerful would it be if a performer had the ability to perceive her own work so clearly that she can read the newspaper review and extract from it only what is useful, without being maimed by the rest?

But let me be clear: I am not advocating simply ignoring the problems in someone's work.

Penetrating the cloud of malaise

The day after her final thesis performance, Karina met with the faculty for feedback. We asked her to talk about what had happened, but as soon as she sat down in the circle, she started crying. She had attempted to make a performance piece that included singing and dance while it also recounted a piece of her personal history. She was deeply disappointed. In her performance, she said, she had taken some risks with her singing, but not as many as she had in rehearsal, and she had not included the dance elements she had planned to; most of all, she had not given herself enough rehearsal time to accomplish what she had set out to do. Finally, she finished her cheerless self-evaluation by saying, "I know I'm just being hard on myself," thus managing to criticize herself for her criticism.

The faculty members in the circle reacted to her distress in different ways: One faculty member sought to comfort her, "I know just what you are feeling. After a recent performance of mine, I also felt devastated. It wasn't so much the show, but the let-down after performance." Another teacher suggested that maybe Karina could show him the dance sections some other time. A third opined that maybe she simply needed more time for herself, and that we did not need to give her feedback now, so soon after yesterday's performance.

My take was different. My feeling was that, while she felt overwhelmed by her negative self-evaluation, the actual content of what she had said was not so monolithically depressing. I suggested that by separating out the various things Karina had mentioned, she might notice that some of her self-criticism—for instance, the choreography never made it into the piece at all—was simply a lesson in the problems of time management, while on the other hand, the questions she raised about the musical sections of her show actually contained exciting information for her—both positive and negative—about her voice work.

I suspected that if she separated out the different elements of what she was saying, she might discover some "criticism" she could actually use.

So I asked her to speak about her experience of those moments on stage when she was singing. As soon as she concentrated on the singing, she noticed that she had, in fact, really enjoyed those moments. With a little exploration, she began to remember that some of the singing itself had been powerful: "I mean I liked working on those extended voice parts. But, of course, I don't know how it was for the audience ... " Her voice trailed off. "I mean, I didn't think the scripted part worked at all."

I asked her to go back and unwrap some more details she could remember about the singing. Now she was able to describe several particularly exciting vocal risks she'd taken, moments of real enjoyment that lay hidden within the miasma of her disappointments. As she spoke, she was able to describe how, in her rehearsals, she'd found herself more and more drawn to the vocal experiments, but that she hadn't allowed herself to "give up" on her grander plans for the piece.

Perhaps I could have begun with my usual, "Name three moments that you liked ... " but in the end, I was glad I had not. The insights Karina came to about what had *not* worked in her piece were intimately connected to what *had* worked. It was actually because the singing had been going well that she had become distracted from seeing that, in order to finish the piece for performance, she would have to shrink her original vision. It wasn't necessary for her to ignore the negative thoughts; what was necessary was for her to rescue the positive and negative details from the cloud of her overall malaise. General feedback (positive or negative) is rarely as meaningful or as useful as specifics. When one is precise, the positive and negative comments will not cancel each other out.

Perceptions and opinions

After helping a student to examine her own work, and after supporting her ability to recall the details of what happened, I do, indeed, make my own comments about what I saw. But even as I do, I try my best to distinguish between what I have *seen* and what my *opinion* is about what I have seen. The physical approach to acting is a great aid in making that distinction for it focuses on what is concrete: actions, gestures, tones of voice rather than on "feelings." In Grotowski's work, what the actor is "doing" are the specific physical choices. The emotions he acts arise involuntarily from those choices.

Thus I might say to a student, "As you approached your scene partner, you were holding your hands behind your back." Or I might point out, "On that line, you began to whisper." Or, "When you turned from left to right, your eyes went to the floor." Sometimes I will point to these things in the form of a question: "Did you notice that as you crossed towards your scene partner your hands were behind your back?" Because, again, more important than my ability to point something out is training the student to perceive her own work. By learning to recall the moment of placing her hands behind her back or of starting to whisper, she is strengthening the mind-muscles she will need to give herself useful feedback in future. If the feedback comes only from me, although it may be accurate and even helpful in that moment, it can leave the student mystified, not knowing how I arrived at what I'm saying.

After I've pointed out what I saw (e.g., "You held your hands behind your back"), then perhaps I'll venture an opinion, "And I kept wondering, what would happen if you reached out for him at that moment?" By separating out "what I saw" from "what seeing that made me think" I leave the student free to disagree with me, in two distinct ways. She can say: "No, that's not what I did" or she can say, "Yes, I did that, but I actually liked that moment. It worked for me." In this way, I try to frame my comments so that she need not feel either her perceptions or her opinions are belittled.

Above all, I will avoid using words like "truth" or "authenticity" because such words are merely opinions masquerading as facts, and as such, they constitute a subtle power-trip. After all, it is almost impossible for a student to disagree with a teacher who tells him his acting is "unbelievable."

More examples and more support

What about those times when I think I know exactly what the student is doing wrong? What if, for instance, I can see that the student is "indicating," putting on a smile for the audience, rather than fully exploring the emotion that is rising within her? At such moments, should I bite my tongue? Should I just leave such moments of "bad acting" alone?

No: but on the other hand, I probably won't say "Don't indicate." If she's "putting on a smile" she's probably doing so because she is already feeling uneasy about the moment. If I tell her she's "indicating," or ask her to "stop smiling" I run the risk of just adding another judgment to the ones she's already experiencing.

So?

Well, I might well urge her in the opposite direction. I might encourage her to exaggerate the smile, let it spread across her whole body, and then to let it go and breathe. Often a habit, a false note, a held expression is actually a defense against something else that is trying to let itself be known. By exaggerating the smile, the defense reveals itself, wears itself out as it were. I wouldn't be surprised if after pushing the smile further and then allowing herself to breathe, the actor might discover that her character was actually on the edge of tears. But, even if I'd suspected that the tears were lurking there below the smile all along, how much more useful it is for the actress to have heard me speak only about exaggerating the smile so that the discovery of the tears is her own.

I've learned to be very careful when helping students become aware of their habits because often students assume that recognizing something as a "habit," is tantamount to labeling it a "bad habit." But actually, a habit often contains interesting information that can be recovered by playing with the habit, not by castigating oneself or simply trying to overcome or change it.

For instance, when I ask students to lie down on the floor on their backs to relax, often a few of them will lie down with their legs crossed at the ankles, and that small physical adjustment can be a subtle way of protecting themselves from becoming completely vulnerable by wholly relaxing against the floor. But if I simply point out to a student that his ankles are crossed, he will quickly uncross them while unconsciously transferring the "holding on" to some less obvious physical location. Now his heels are both on the floor, but the information that was contained in the crossed ankles, the emotional content of that habitual gesture, is hidden even farther out of reach.

So I've learned that when I notice those crossed ankles, I should approach the student and softly say, "Now as I speak, let yourself listen to what I'm saying, but don't feel you must change what you are doing." Then I may touch his ankles and add, "Now feel what your ankles are doing. And now, as you continue to lie there, take some time exploring what this little gesture here is about. Play with the ankles; maybe move them against each other, try crossing and uncrossing them several times. And see if you can discover what they are doing for you."

Exploring the habit, rather than trying to eliminate it, the student may discover that this is a habit that he really needs at this point in the work, but at least now he can cross those ankles on purpose, sensing the comfort and safety this gesture affords him. Or perhaps, through his exploration, he will find that he can obtain the comfort he craves in some other way. In either case, he has converted an unconscious habit into a conscious action. What was a habit is now a choice, and the energy contained in that habit is now energy he can use.

Sometimes, when I think I know just what a student must do to solve a problem, rather than offering the "solution," I'll suggest several possibilities she might try, so that she can find out which one works by experimentation. For instance, if I suspect that a student is not giving herself permission to freely express the anger her character is experiencing, I might say, "Well, if the line doesn't feel right, you could try screaming it, or whispering it, or saying it between clenched teeth. If you experiment with strong choices, the right one will usually become clear." (And if she comes out preferring a different choice than the one I would have made, then I must support that choice, suspecting that at a later rehearsal, she may change her mind.) Biology teacher Robert Zull offers a similar idea:

> When it comes to learning, self-evaluation is more useful than the teacher's evaluation. The teacher should just stick to her role of challenge and support. When she is dissatisfied with her student, instead of placing value on the work, she should provide more examples and more support. Evaluation can support learning only when the student requests it.
>
> (Zull, 2002, p. 242)

So what I'm suggesting is not that the teacher must eschew giving feedback, but rather that she should do her best to give the feedback in a form that will not interfere with the student's own discovery process. Sometimes, I've discovered, that means I must even abandon my penchant for the positive.

Non-interference

One day, when I announced to my acting class that we would be working on monologues, a young actress in the class said she wanted to try Blanche, from Tennessee Williams' *A Streetcar Named Desire*. This young woman had been struggling all semester with problems of fear, hesitation, and control, personal psychological habits that had, for years, been artistic blocks in her work. So I had some hesitation about letting her undertake the speech. I thought it might be an enormous stretch for her, such a stretch that she might end up feeling defeated, which would definitely not be a helpful experience for her. On the other hand, I knew that the role would push her physically and emotionally in directions that could be important for her: openness, wonder, sexuality, and freedom with her movements. So I said, okay.

Blanche's monologue is a fantasy about drinking and swimming in the old rock quarry. The first time through, the actress looked down at the floor in front of her most of the time. As she spoke to Blanche's imaginary friends, she took furtive glances out towards the imagery, but her voice was very quiet, her expression tentative. Not very Blanche-like at all. After the scene ended, she said she was not happy with what she had done with the monologue. That's all she would say, so rather than agree or disagree with her assessment, I thought it best to just suggest a couple of simple, physical things she could try, to find out what difference they might make to the performance and to her own acting experience. I suggested she try placing the image of the rock quarry farther off, behind the audience, and that she simply speak in a louder voice. The second time through, she made those adjustments, and it seemed to me that when she did, her eyes lit up, and her face assumed a seductive smile. I was certainly more convinced that her Blanche might really have such a reverie.

So, when she finished the monologue this second time, I asked her: "How was that?" She didn't answer. So I refined my question, "How did you feel doing that?"

"Weird," she answered.

"Just weird?" I asked.

"I don't know. What do you mean?" she asked.

"Well," I said, "since what you just did was new and different for you, it is natural that you might feel 'weird,' but did you have any other sensation or perception besides that it felt weird?"

She responded: "I feel like you want me to say something."

It was a wonderful lesson—for me. I had perceived, or thought I had perceived, some real enjoyment and even some sensuality in her monologue this second time. But having watched her work for many weeks, I knew that, for this young woman, "enjoyment" and "sensuality" were not mentionable conditions. She was a woman who had built her self-image and her acting ability around strength, hard work, and apparent fearlessness. Anger she could handle. But enjoyment and sensuality never showed themselves in her work.

So, by even hinting to her that I had perceived something there, something behind the "weirdness" she was experiencing in her work, I was putting her in a terrible position. "Weird" was her word, and I was forcing her to choose between her own sense of honesty and capitulating to a received truth. If I were then to lead her, step by step—as I probably could have—to say, "I felt excitement" or "enjoyment" or maybe even "sensuality," her admission would carry within it the self-statement: " ... and I am stupid not to have perceived that." The truth in that moment was that what the teacher perceived was irrelevant to her process. In fact it would be inimical to it because it would interrupt *her* learning, a process that depended upon her gaining both self-perception and self-confidence.

If my words undermined her feelings of self-worth, or made her feel "You want me to say something," they would deprive her of the most important things she was learning. My question to her: "Did you have any other sensation ... ?" sounded to her—quite rightly—like one of those rhetorical non-questions the teacher asks, knowing what the "right" answer is. She was letting me know that, at that moment, she did not want to be coerced into accepting my vision of her work. I, on the other hand, felt caught and didn't quite know what to do. I only knew I needed to step back because, behind her words, I felt she was telling me: "You are invading my process. I need more room, more space to discover this for myself."

So I stumbled around for words that would not deprive her of her "truth." Some way to let her have her word, "weird," and yet to leave the door open.

"You have been working all semester," I began, "with questions like how can you feel safe taking up more space, moving away from the wall, and using your voice more strongly. So it is perfectly natural that it might feel weird when you start to do so. But," I added, "often one can feel more than one thing at the same time. So even while you, the actor, were feeling 'weird,' it is possible that at the same time, the character, Blanche, might be having another experience." She nodded and we left it at that.

I went home that day wondering if I had said the right thing. Perhaps I'd said too much, implying that she ought to be able to perceive what I perceived within her work. Or perhaps I'd said too little, and with a few well-chosen words could have led her to take possession of the power and sensuality that Blanche's monologue had begun to evoke in her.

The next time this student came into class she took me aside and said, "You know I'm in a show now, and I'm playing a character who is really very sexy. And last night while I was on stage it occurred to me that Blanche could feel like that too. I don't know why that didn't occur to me before." Having come to that insight outside of class and on her own, it was a discovery that was entirely "hers," not something she'd received from the teacher. I was surprised, and gratified. I couldn't know whether her discovery was connected with the work she'd done in my class, but at least I was reassured that I had not bent her learning curve to my schedule. It seems I had stepped back far enough for her to take the next steps in her process in her own time.

Of course this kind of "stepping back" can be hard for a teacher. With this student it meant biting my tongue and foregoing the pleasure of sounding wise or insightful. But I account the loss well compensated by the pleasure of witnessing a student gaining confidence in her own work.

When and where

So far, we've been talking about *what*—what to say when giving feedback. But there are other issues too, such as *where* and *when* to say it.

As I've said, when we're sitting in a circle after a group exercise, I will often ask my students to describe their experiences in the work. When I began teaching, I enjoyed responding to each student after he or she spoke, proud that I had something insightful to say to everyone. Nowadays I do that less and less often, instead reserving what I have to say for the very end, after everyone has spoken, for several reasons: First of all, I realized that if I chimed in after each student, the continuity of the process would be lost. Second, each comment I made would affect what those who had yet to speak might want to say. If I interrupted the reflections with my own comments, pointing out, perhaps, that what the last speaker said was "interesting" or "insightful," the following speaker might hesitate to describe her own, very different experience, thus narrowing the range of responses we might hear. Since one of the lessons I'm aiming at in such moments is that many people, each having done exactly the same exercise, might have completely different experiences, my comments would tend to undercut the very purpose of the work. Finally, it often happens that by the time the circle is complete, other students have come up with the same thoughts I might have had myself. Saving my comments for the end allows me to point out similarities, themes, and deeper lessons that draw together different students' experiences—and sometimes it allows me to say nothing at all because everything that needed to be said has been said by the students. At the end of several circles recently I've found myself saying simply: "I have nothing to say. Really, you've covered it all. Thank you." This sort of comment from a teacher can come as a slight shock or even a disappointment to students at first, but it's a disappointment with a silver lining: The realization that they are, indeed, becoming their own teachers.

Then there's the *where* question. Whenever possible, I will try to transform my feedback to individual actors into feedback for the whole group. For instance, after a student has presented a scene and we've analyzed a difficulty the student was encountering (say, avoiding looking downstage towards the audience), I often find myself turning out to the rest of the group to provide context. "Many actors run into this same problem, but it is a wonderful thing to discover, as Brady did just now, that the energy of 'stage fright' can actually be of use to the actor within the scene." This gambit has several advantages. For one, it lets the student whose work we've been observing feel he's not alone in the difficulty he's been encountering. Also, especially if I've been working for many minutes with this one student, it lets the others know they're not forgotten.

On the other hand, some kinds of feedback are better offered privately. When I suspect that an actor is running into strong personal material, or when an actor's behavior seems to be having ill effects upon the group, it's usually safer to talk about it with the student privately. Many years ago, one student had a particularly self-revelatory way of joking about herself. Her sly innuendos about her sexual activities over the weekend didn't bother me, but as I looked around the circle, it looked to me like her brash style was off-putting to many of the other students. It was not the kind of thing I wanted to mention with everyone there, so I met with her privately. She said she'd been wondering why no one was working with her in the warm-up and that she had no idea that her way of speaking was off-putting. A word to the wise was sufficient.

Sometimes when I've sensed that a student might need to talk, I've scheduled a private conference and been told that whatever was going on was not something the student wanted to share, and that was that. But at other times it has turned out that the student did need to talk—about something they didn't think was relevant to the class, such as that they had been finding life in New York City enormously unpleasant. Our private conference allowed them to say out loud what they'd been thinking: "This city drives me nuts. Why does everybody else seem to like it so much?"

Another situation in which I try to avoid public feedback is when I feel that this is the moment to give an actor some particularly strong praise for the work he did. Often it can be delightful for the full group to acknowledge that someone who has been struggling has suddenly broken free. But that depends not just on the one student, but on the condition of the whole group. If some members of the class are apt to denigrate their own work by comparing it to others', then giving public praise to one student could have a negative effect on others; such compliments may best be shared with the student after class. Of course, it would be wonderful if we were all immune to comparison, competiveness, and envy. But we ain't.[2]

Student feedback

What about students giving other students feedback on their work? I've changed my opinion about this over the years. Early on in my teaching,

2 Sharon Salzberg and other Buddhist teachers encourage the practice of *mudita*, the ability to take joy in another's happiness. Not easy. Often not easy at all.

after the first round of scenes was complete, I would often encourage my students to give feedback to the other students in the class during the second round of scenes. I'd begin by having the actors who had just worked speak, but then, before I said my piece, I'd ask for comments from the rest of the class. I rarely do this anymore for I found that, although some students had clear, helpful things to say, other students' comments often ran along the lines of, "What I really wanted you to do at that moment was ... " Or "Why didn't you ... ?" They were commenting as actors, talking about what *they* would do if they were working on the scene rather than helping the student who had just worked figure it out for himself. I realized that asking students to suddenly step out of their acting personae to think like a teacher was not really helpful—for them or for the student who had just worked.

On the other hand, for the past six years I've been teaching graduate students, many of whom plan to become teachers of acting or singing or movement themselves. With them, I've started leading a "pedagogy" class in which everyone takes a turn teaching—anything they'd like to teach—and then the whole group discusses the lesson and gives the student-teacher feedback about their teaching. In this class, I urge students to notice precisely what the student-teacher does: How did he introduce the work? Did the progression of exercises work for you? Did the leader create a safe working environment? Did his tone of voice and vocabulary aid or undermine the learning experience? Then, when the "lesson" is over, I have the student-teacher talk first about her own perceptions, and then I ask the others to offer their feedback.

A couple of years ago a student in one of those pedagogy classes summed up the central thing I've been trying to say in this chapter. Sandor was always an insightful observer, and that day he was particularly accurate with his feedback, putting his finger on exactly what it was that had disturbed him about another student's lesson. After he'd said what he had so say, and then had rephrased it to be even more precise, the student he was addressing—the woman who had led the lesson—was clearly on the edge of tears. She asked if we could take a break, and after we all returned, it took the group several minutes of processing to re-open the listening space that Sandor's perspicuity had so suddenly closed down. At the end of the process, Sandor spoke up once more, "I think I just understood something about the difference between being right and being helpful."

For anyone teaching or offering feedback, there is a terrible temptation to share one's insight and one's wisdom. After years of teaching, it is, indeed, true that I know some things, and can sometimes give a student a useful push in the right direction. Often enough, in fact, it would be fairly easy for me to point out what an actor should do to correct a problem he's running into. Easy, but not nearly as educational as helping the actor figure it out for himself. So my strong conviction remains that I must resist that temptation, at least long enough to consider whether, if I keep my peace, the student might just figure the problem out for himself. As Eloise Ristad points out, this can also be true when teaching "technique":

> If a student is part of the process of discovery—finding a fingering that works well, finding how important a flexible wrist is, discovering how to keep an arm relaxed on octaves—the solution to a problem then becomes a personal triumph. The solution becomes a self-given gift—a gift that means a welcome short-cut in learning this wonderful new piece. Because of that gift, the student is then more ready to accept the gift of my additional insight, or the insight of someone else in the group. Gifts that come only from outside sources not only make us lazy but also resentful and rebellious. The gift of a teacher's wisdom too feely bestowed becomes a burden.
>
> (Ristad, 1982, p. 132)

Here Ristad confirms what I was trying to say in the chapter on the *via negativa*: that what we're talking about here is not a matter of giving up the teaching of technique, but rather the patience to hold off the technique lesson until the "teachable moment" arises, the moment when that lesson will not undermine the student's sense of "personal triumph."

So now let us turn to some stickier teaching situations: What is a teacher to do when such "teachable moments" never seem to arise because a student is actively resisting what one has to teach? And how should we react to those students who seem determined not to learn?

Chapter 6

Resistance

There are no resistant patients, only incompetent therapists.

Jay Haley

For one semester, Eric had been guest-teaching a movement class in our department, and the word on him from the students in the hallway was mixed. Some students said his classes were exciting, but others grumbled that he just didn't "get it." At the end-of-semester teachers' meeting, I got an inkling of what "it" was.

"I'm sorry," Eric began, when the department chair asked for his comments at the meeting, "but this is just the laziest group of students I've ever worked with. I expect students to come into the studio ready to work. But these ... I felt like I had to prove something to them. You know, I've been teaching dance since before some of these kids were born. Why are they doing this to me?"

After some back-and-forth with the other teachers, it became clear that Eric had never before taught in a theater department. He'd always taught in dance departments, and he found the kinds of questions these theater students had pestered him with simply irrelevant to his work. "It seems like they all want to know, 'why, why, why?' That's not the way I teach. You don't talk about the work, you *do* the work. If they don't want to do the work, what are they doing in school?" At the end of the meeting, Eric summed up his diagnosis. "You know what I think it is? I think it's not laziness. It's resistance."

"Resistance" is a word borrowed from psychoanalysis where it refers to the way in which a patient can unconsciously "resist" the analyst's efforts to free him from his neuroses. But as psychologist James Krantz points out, "The concept of resistance ... has been transformed over the years into a not-so-disguised way of blaming the less powerful for unsatisfactory results of change efforts" (Krantz, 1999, p. 42). In other words, resistance can be a "problem" when the therapist sees it as a problem, rather than as a clue as to how this particular client experiences the world.

The situation is similar in the classroom, for oftentimes teachers have a hard time seeing "disruptive" behavior as anything but an affront.

The biggest obstacle

Parker Palmer is a teacher who has thought a great deal about teaching, and in his insightful book, *The Courage to Teach, Exploring the Inner Landscape of a Teacher's Life,* he gives evidence that Eric was not alone in his grievance:

> When I ask teachers to name the biggest obstacle to good teaching, the answer I most often hear is "my students." When I ask why this is so, I hear a litany of complaints: my students are silent, sullen, withdrawn; they have little capacity for conversation; they have short attention spans; they do not engage well with ideas; they cling to narrow notions of "relevance" and "usefulness" and dismiss the world of ideas.
>
> (Palmer, 1998, p. 40)

If Eric had heard these other teachers' complaints, he would probably have agreed: The obstacle to his teaching was the students. The teachers Palmer spoke to would probably have agreed with Eric that their students' behaviors were all symptoms of one epidemic disease: Resistance.

What gets called "resistance," however, shows up in many forms, from laziness or sullenness to out-and-out refusal to learn. Let's begin by talking about the less virulent forms, and then work our way up.

Symptomatology

First of all, we should note that what seems like resistance can actually be a symptom of some personal difficulty a student is having. Sometimes identical "symptoms" bespeak completely different underlying dis-eases and therefore require completely different interventions. This is a lesson I learned the hard way.

My education on this issue began during my second year as a university acting teacher. One of my students seemed to be falling asleep in class—often. I had tried talking to the whole group about "being present." I had taken this young man aside in class and told him I was noticing. But it kept happening. Not all the time, but often enough. Too often.

He was a good actor, and when he was working, he seemed eager to learn. I'm not a confrontational person, so I held off. Sometimes I'd tap him on the shoulder to wake him up. Sometimes I'd just fix my gaze on him. Finally, I told him to come see me after class.

When I asked him what's going on, he squirmed, he evaded, and then he admitted he'd been partying 'till all hours most weekends. I told him that it was his choice: He simply had to choose between partying and studying acting. He looked abashed. After that short discussion, he was wide awake, and he did some terrific scene work. At the end of the semester, he thanked me and said he'd learned a lot. I thought I'd learned something too. I was wrong.

The next semester—different student, same pattern. This time I knew what to do. The second time it happened, I invited the young woman into my office. "You've got to choose," I said, "between studying acting and whatever else you're doing on the weekends." Suddenly she was in tears. For a minute she could barely speak. When she'd recovered, she explained that she was a work-study student and that after school she had to work in the library until 11 every evening, and then start her academic homework.

"I just need a day off," she sobbed. "One day to catch up."

"Does your scene go up tomorrow?"

"No, not until Friday."

"If you skip class tomorrow, can you take a nap?"

"Skip class? Your class?"

"Yes."

She missed that one day. Friday she seemed in much better shape. Later in the semester, she asked whether she could miss one more day. I said okay. Her final scene presentation was terrific. We'd both learned our lessons, I thought.

It wasn't until two years later that I had another sleepy student in my class. This time I tried to apply what I'd learned. I took the student aside at the end of class and asked him what was going on, perhaps, I suggested, he needed to take a day off.

Suddenly he flew into a rage. Why should he take a day off? Wasn't that the problem in the first place? Didn't I remember, he'd missed the first two days of class because of his accident? (I'd forgotten.) I'd never filled him in on what he missed those days, so he was always thinking everyone else in class knew something he didn't, but since I hadn't explained it, he figured he was supposed to work it out for himself. He wasn't tired, really, he was just anxious all the time. And now I wanted him to take a day off?!

I offered to meet with him for an hour after class the next day, go over what he'd missed and answer any questions he had. He never looked sleepy in class again. But I had to really take stock. Why, I wondered, was I always "fighting the last war."

My stumbling attempts to learn from past mistakes put me in mind of the sad irony of taking at face value Santayana's line, "Those who cannot remember the past are condemned to repeat it" (Santayana, 1905, p. 284). Several years ago, I was one of several writers working on *The People's Temple*, a play about Jim Jones and Jonestown, the communal utopia Jones and his followers founded in Guyana in the 1970s. Santayana's famous line was written on a placard that hung above their meeting hall. It was their shibboleth, and it hung there on the day in 1978 when 914 of the commune members committed suicide—or were murdered—depending on how you read the history.

The problem with learning from what you remember of the past is that history is made up of events, not lessons. The lessons we take are what we *infer* from history, but they may not be the right ones.

So, in three different classes I had had three different students, each of whom exhibited the same symptom of what I took to be "resistance." But for each one, that symptom had a completely different etiology, and it necessitated a completely different treatment. In each of these instances, their "resistance" turned out not to be resistance at all but some life-problem that I had just misread.

Varieties of resistance

There are, however, situations in which students are genuinely resistant to the lesson one is trying to teach. Let's begin with the easy cases: One simple form of resistance—maybe what Eric was encountering in his dance class—is "testing." Students often—and sometimes for good reason—are wary of new teachers and need some reassurance. Some just want to check out what it is that the teacher has to teach them, some need to feel that they are seen, and some want to be sure that this teacher is not like the teacher who demeaned their work six years ago.

To pass the "test" a teacher may need real patience, for the student wants to sense that the teacher will "be there" for the student, even when the student is difficult. It also helps if you can figure out what the student actually needs from you. Once I found that a student who seemed distant opened up more after I mentioned the World Series game in class. Other students have clearly appreciated my talking about my own struggles as an acting student. The apparent content of the test is never the issue; the essence of what each student was "testing" was my ability to "see" who they are and sense what they need.

Another thing that can appear to be "resistance" is simply fear: fear of the unknown, of a new group or of a new way of working. Ruthie is a dancer who has been teaching and choreographing dances for many years. She tells this story:

> I was working on a new piece with four dancers, a dance piece that included speaking too. And one of the dancers I had cast was a woman I'd never worked with before. I'd seen her in other people's work. She moved well, and in a couple of those pieces she had spoken with a really strong voice, like booming. So anyway, we'd been working for about a week, and I had explained to the group that in this one section, I wanted them to just turn out to the audience and say whatever they happened to be thinking at that moment. It could be about their movements, or about the audience, or that they'd just remembered that they'd left the water running back home. Whatever. But every run-through this new dancer would say the same thing. Some line about her teddy bear. So after the third time this happened I took her aside and I said, "You can't be really thinking about that damned bear (I don't think I said damned) that much. Just say what you're thinking at that moment." And she said she would try, and sure enough, the next time through, she didn't talk about the teddy bear. She talked about a stork, some kind of toy stork! I mean she was doing all the move-ment stuff just fine, but the stork line like came out sounding just as memorized as the bear one had. And I'm thinking, this woman is just being difficult, I'm going to have to replace her. I was really pissed and I said, "What's going on? That line about the stork was clearly not what you were thinking. It sounded rehearsed." And then she was like on the edge of tears, and she said, "But what if I don't have anything to say?" So I said, "But how did you say what you just said? How did you say, 'But what if I don't have anything to say?'" And she looked at me like she'd seen a ghost, and she said, "But that's ... I would be terrified to be out there with no words at all and. ... " "Yeah," I said, "then that's what you say. If that's what you're thinking, you just say that, 'I'm terrified.'" And she did. And that was it. After that day, her verbal improvs were often very interesting. Sometimes she came out with these totally off-the-wall lines. So I was just wrong. She wasn't being difficult. She was just afraid of trying something new.

Fear, as I suggested in the chapter on Questioning, has a bad rep, so very few students will come right out and say, "I'm scared." Many might not even be aware that fear is what is going on for them. Most will have invented clever disguises for their fear, so that they need not acknowledge it, even to themselves. It may look at first like aggression, or sleepiness, or distraction. But it will often "speak" in clear, non-verbal ways. For instance, fear will show itself in where a student chooses to work in the room, or in the direction he faces, or in whether or not he makes eye contact.

The student who always chooses to work up against the rear wall of the studio is telling me something about his state of mind. The student who always sneaks a look at the teacher and the student who never looks at the teacher at all are also letting me know what they are feeling. The student who complains about an exercise—like the one who says, "Why are we doing these exercises anyway?"—is simultaneously giving me information, if only I can read it as such. Even the student who refuses to reveal himself in the work reveals himself in his style of refusal. The important thing is that I be able to listen to a complaint *about* an exercise as openly as I can watch the work *within* an exercise.

Wrestling and aikido

So now, let us return to the question we postponed a couple of chapters back: The case of the student who asks after the Cat exercise, "Why are we doing this anyway?" but does not accept my, "That's a good question. I wonder if you can live with that question for a while without needing to have an answer ... " as a useful challenge. The student who cannot perceive that having "a good question" is exactly the point.

Well, I might try pointing out to him that the Cat exercise is designed to provoke just such feelings, but that it also provides a form inside of which one can transform such feelings into acting choices. I might say, "It sounds to me like one of the things you experienced in the exercise was frustration. But you know, one of the central reasons we are doing this exercise is to learn how to use things like frustration when they appear."

But then, what if his response to this gambit is along the lines of, "Oh, don't give me that bullshit! You're just trying to get me angry with you, right?"

Well okay. I'm being challenged directly now, and the chief thing is that I do not take this challenge as a personal attack—even if, or rather especially if—that is how it is meant: for my task is to help the student perceive that even a personal challenge is a workable artistic source. So, when a student comes right out and confronts me like that, I must do my best to turn his vehemence to good use. In a situation like this,

I might suspect that the anger this student is experiencing has something to do with whatever happened to him during the Cat exercise, and/or that this anger is actually deeply rooted in his personal history. But neither of these suspicions is relevant right now. This is an acting training class, not a therapy session, so the *source* of his anger is not the point. The point is to help this student comprehend that the frustration and anger he is experiencing, even something that feels to him to be "outside the work"—like rage at the teacher—can be put to good use and funneled into the work. So whether or not his anger has very deep roots, what matters is that the experience he is in touch with right now is that he is angry at *me*. So that's what I've got to work with. Moreover, the fact that he is willing to be so open with his anger at me signals that, in a way, *he is already working with me.* My job is just to help him see that.

So, I might ask him if he is willing to get up, right then, and work with me, perhaps doing a "back-to-back" exercise, pushing against each other with our backs, exploring various rhythms and emotions as we move around the room. (The interesting thing to note here is that students who express this kind of direct challenge to the teacher are also hungry for special attention, and usually quite willing to jump in!) In the back-to-back exercise, this student will get the immediate—and satisfying—experience of embodying the very feelings he is having: anger at the teacher. So the fact that he has dared to voice this emotion is a great opportunity to let him discover how a formal, physical "container"—like working with his legs and back—can allow him to use the energy flowing through him—even when it seems to be the energy of an opinion *about* the work. In this work, his "resistance" *to* the work is transformed directly into a part *of* the work, and his disgust at my non-answers is turned into an exciting "teachable moment."

The delightful thing about working with resistance in this way is that the problem—in this case the student's mistrust of the teacher—becomes the very foundation of the solution. Moreover, the student himself (and the others watching) can see that it is just fine to confront me, and that emotions—even "impermissible" ones, like anger at the teacher—are quite permissible in this class, and that I will not reject someone simply because he gets enraged at me or at the work.

Over the years, I've grown quite accustomed to the occasional flashes of anger-at-the-teacher that can appear as a student struggles with an exercise that runs her headlong into her blocks. So these days, when someone reacts against a suggestion of mine or growls, "I hate you," in the midst of her work, I find myself inwardly smiling, for the outburst is a sign of her willingness to work hard, a sign of her growing awareness of exactly what she is feeling in the moment, and a sign of the trust she feels in me and in the work, the trust that allows her to say such a thing out loud.

But sometimes wrestling directly with a student's antagonism is not what's called for. With some kinds of resistance, I have found that the most effective strategy is less like wrestling and more like aikido: stepping out of the way and making room for the resistance to wear itself out.

Several years ago, I was teaching a "Boundless Improvisation" class, an improvisation format that movement teacher Wendell Beavers and I had developed, in which we combined theater games with improv forms from dance and singing to build a thoroughly interdisciplinary performance investigation. In each Boundless Improv class session, the group would study another form: Six Viewpoints, a theater game, or a vocal improv form, and then we'd try to add the new form to our constantly expanding improv vocabulary. Each day, before undertaking the new material, I'd ask the class to begin with an open warm-up, 15 minutes during which the students reconnected their bodies and voices, made contact with each other, and practiced the skills we'd accumulated during the previous classes.

Lila was a young woman who had been doing improvisations since she was 13. She wanted to learn the new forms, but she hated the warm-up. "I've been doing warm-ups for years. It's boring. Boring!" Her pouting tone sounded to me like a challenge: I don't want to do this, and I bet you can't make me.

So I said, "That's fine. You don't have to take part in the warm-up. You have to be here, but you can just watch. Okay?"

"Okay," she said, doubtfully.

For a week Lila sat out while the rest of the class warmed up. She watched them playing with each other, singing, getting better at the improvs, having fun. Finally, one day, she just couldn't take it anymore. She didn't say anything, she just got out on the floor with the others and joined in.

Lila's refusal to participate in the warm-up had been her way of saying, "Make me do it." When I told her she could sit out and watch, it was not my clever way of getting her to join. (I'm not that smart.) At that moment all I knew was I was being challenged, and I suspected that if I forced her to join in the warm-up, then for the remainder of the seven week class, she could have said to herself: "I'm only doing this because the teacher made me." By allowing her the freedom to make up her own mind, I was giving her two messages. One was: "I respect you and your ability to choose what to do." The other was the corollary: "Whatever you choose is your responsibility." Lila may have learned a little bit about improv during the semester, but I suspect that her biggest learning took place in this little dance she and I performed about her participation in the warm-up.

Then there was Ezra, a student who seemed to have worked out the perfect trap for himself. He was a very strong actor who could do very detailed movement and character work, and he had a crackling sense of humor, but on occasion, Ezra would act so aggressively towards the other class members that fewer and fewer people were willing to work with him. Then, feeling rejected by the other students, he would become sullen because—he confided to me privately one day—nobody liked him. When he hit one of his dark moods, he might just disappear for a day or two with no explanation. Other teachers were at the ends of their ropes with him, and when several of his fellow students complained to the administration about Ezra's furious outbursts, the faculty initiated the process—official warnings, meetings with the dean—that would permit the department to throw him out of school.

I suspected, however, that behind this young man's periodic waves of bluster, there lay an enormous sea of insecurity, one that he hid—quite effectively—by acting belligerent. After many false starts, I discovered that what he needed was constant reassurance that he was seen and appreciated. If I gave Ezra enthusiastic praise every time he opened himself to the work or to others, his inner panic would abate, and his hostile outbursts would recede. Of course there were days when that could be a very difficult thing to do, like those days when he would simply stop working or start to curse under his breath. On such days I'd catch myself about to reprimand him as I was sucked into the dark cloud of negative energy he exuded, but then I'd remind myself to breathe, and I'd find something—a joke, a slap on the back, or a hug—that could bring him (and me) out of the gloom. When it was clear that this approach really helped, I spoke about it with the other teachers, and collectively we were able to step back from the brink and support Ezra in his zig-zag progress in school.

To sum up: Whenever resistance crops up, we must not ignore it or let it slide, but we must also avoid letting it control us. We must try to see it as an opportunity, a coded signal about what a student needs from us. Sometimes what he needs is to be pushed to do something he's refusing to do, but more often what he needs is help in witnessing and learning from his own recalcitrance.

Then, of course, there are those situations when, in spite of our best efforts, a student's behavior just drives us nuts.

Chapter 7

Transference

> What are transferences? They are new editions or facsimiles of the impulses and phantasies which are aroused and made conscious during the progress of the analysis; but they have this peculiarity, which is characteristic for their species, that they replace some earlier person by the person of the physician.
>
> Sigmund Freud

At the Experimental Theatre Wing at NYU, where I taught for over 20 years, the teachers all share a room with a sign on the door that reads "Teacher Lounge." That's a euphemism. The lounge is a sunless room with a couch, a couple of computers, and two walls lined with lockers. Since the Experimental Theatre Wing is a body-centered acting studio, for most of teachers it serves as a changing room into and out of their sweaty work clothes before and after classes. Others use the room for semi-private conversations with students. Occasionally a teacher will try to sleep on the couch, but that's not easy with all the coming and going.

One day, years ago, I was trying to rest on the couch to recover sufficiently from one class to be able to face the next one. I'd almost fallen asleep when the door to the lounge slammed shut, hard. I opened my eyes and saw Christopher, the new voice teacher, standing in the middle of the room, glaring at the two locker-lined walls, looking back and forth, as if he were trying to decide which one to punch.

I sat up.

"Sorry," said Christopher, "I didn't see you."

"That's okay," I said. I didn't know Christopher well. I knew many students found his classes exciting. I knew his singing students' performances were strong. But he had a reputation for flying off the handle sometimes in class.

"Something happened?" I asked. It was pretty obvious.

"No. Yes. Kato. Fucking Kato. I'd like to … " He didn't finish the sentence.

Kato was a tough kid: I mean literally. He had jet-black dyed hair, wore a nose ring, knee-high boots, and a black leather jacket. Although he was probably just 18, he could give you the impression he'd seen more of life than you had—and maybe he had.

"What?" I asked.

"For the umpteenth time, I told him to take off those goddamned boots. How the hell is he supposed to do a voice warm-up in those boots?"

"And, he wouldn't?"

"Oh, he took off his boots! And then he took off that goddamned jacket, and then he took off his pants, and his shirt, and his undershirt. And he stood there in his boxer shorts, which were covered with red polka-dots. And I just lost it."

"What did you do?"

"I ordered him out of the class."

"In his boxers?"

"Yeah. And when I opened the door, he was headed down the hall. And by the time I caught up with him, he was going down the stairs toward the street."

"What did you do?"

"What could I do? He had me beat. I handed him back his clothes and asked him to come back into the class."

"And did he?"

"He did. And he smiled this goddamned, smarmy smile all through the class. I could kill him." Christopher slammed his locker door closed, twice. "I could just kill him."

Christopher was right. Kato had him beat. Christopher slammed the locker one more time and sat down. I didn't know what to say. Then I thought of my experience with Lila, how I'd stepped back to give her room instead of answering her challenge. But when I started recounting the Lila story to him, Christopher just glared at me. I wasn't being helpful. I had just slipped back into my habit of trying to fix the situation. I shut up.

But for weeks after that day, I wondered: what had happened between Christopher and Kato, and what should a teacher do in such a situation?

The student from hell

In *The Courage to Teach,* Parker Palmer tells a story he calls "The Student from Hell," in which he describes quite precisely how a student's learning style can undermine a teacher. Here's the story in its entirety:

> I had just finished a two-day faculty workshop on a Midwestern university campus. Amid high praise for the work we had done together—which, I was told, had given people deeper insight into the pedagogical arts—I was ushered into a political science class where I had agreed to be "teacher for an hour."
> I should have left while the leaving was good.
> There were thirty students in that classroom. It is possible that twenty-nine of them were ready to learn, but I will never know. For in the back row, in the far corner, slouched the specter called the Student from Hell.
> The Student from Hell is a universal archetype that can take male or female form; mine happened to be male. His cap was pulled down over his eyes so that I could not tell whether they were open or shut. His notebooks and writing instruments were nowhere to be seen. It was a fine spring day, but his jacket was buttoned tight, signifying readiness to bolt at any moment.
> What I remember most vividly is his posture. Though he sat in one of those sadistic classroom chairs with a rigidly attached desk, he had achieved a position that I know to be anatomically impossible: despite the interposed desk, his body was parallel to the floor. Seeking desperately to find even one redeeming feature in the specter before me, I seized on the idea that he must practice the discipline of hatha yoga to be able to distort his body so completely.
> At that point in my life, I had been teaching for twenty-five years. Yet faced with the Student from Hell, I committed the most basic mistake of the greenest neophyte: I became totally obsessed with him, and everyone else in the room disappeared from my screen.
> For a long and anguished hour I aimed everything I had at this young man, trying desperately to awaken him from his dogmatic slumbers, but the harder I tried, the more he seemed to recede. Meanwhile, the other students became ciphers as my obsession with the Student from Hell made me oblivious to their needs. I learned that day what a black hole is: a place where the gravity is so intense that all traces of light disappear.
> I left that class with a powerful combination of feelings; self-pity, fraudulence, and rage. On the heels of a highly touted workshop on teaching, I had put on a stunningly inept demonstration of the art. The regular teacher had taken my presence as an excuse to skip his

own class, so my travesty had gone unobserved by any peer, as usual. But my self-respect was gravely wounded, and I knew whom to blame: it was the fault of the Student from Hell. Self-pity and projected blame—the recipe for a well-lived life!

I was desperate to get out of town, but I had to suffer through one more event, dinner with a few faculty at the president's house. There, the workshop received fresh praise, but now the praise was painful, driving me deeper into feelings of fraudulence. When the president announced the arrival of the college van that would haul me to the airport, I was flooded with relief.

I went out to the driveway, tossed my bags into the back seat of the van, climbed into the front seat, and turned to greet the driver.

It was the Student from Hell.

I am a religious person, so I commenced to pray: "I have sinned, I do sin, and given attractive opportunity, I will probably sin again. But nothing I have ever done or plan to merits this punishment—an hour and a half in a van with the Student from Hell."

We backed out of the driveway and wound our way through the neighborhood, staring ahead in silence. When we reached the freeway, the driver suddenly spoke: "Dr. Palmer, is it OK if we talk?"

Every atom in my body screamed "No!" but my mouth, which was trained in the suburbs, said, "Sure, fine, yes, you bet."

I will always remember the conversation that followed. The student's father was an unemployed laborer and an alcoholic who thought that his son's desire to finish college and become some sort of professional was utter nonsense.

The young man lived with his father, who berated him daily for his foolishness: "The world is out to get people like us, and college is part of the scam. Drop out, get a fast-food job, save whatever you can, and settle for it. That's how it'll always be."

Daily this young man felt his motivation for college fading away. "Have you ever been in a situation like this?" he asked. "What do you think I should do about it?"

We talked until it was time for my plane to take off, and for a while afterward we corresponded. I do not know whether I helped him—but I know he helped me. He helped me understand the silent and seemingly sullen students in our classrooms are not brain-dead: they are full of fear.

The Student from Hell is not born that way but is created by conditions beyond his or her control.

(Palmer, 1998, pp. 42–44)

After relating this cautionary tale, Palmer adds this final comment:

> Why do we have so much trouble seeing students as they really are?
> Why do we diagnose their condition in morbid terms that lead to
> deadly modes of teaching? Why do we not see the fear that is in
> their hearts and find ways to help them through it, rather than
> accusing them of being ignorant and banal?
>
> On one level, the answer is simple: our conventional diagnosis
> allows us to ignore our failings as teachers by blaming our victims. But
> there is a deeper reason for our blindness to our students' fears, and
> it is more daunting: we cannot see the fear in our students until we see
> the fear in ourselves. When we deny our own condition, we resist
> seeing anything in others that might remind us of who, and how,
> *we* really are.
>
> If you were reading between the lines of my story of the Student
> from Hell, you know that there are two morals to that tale. One is
> about the fear of the student; the other is about the fear within me.
>
> (Palmer, 1998, p. 47)

Palmer's view, that "we cannot see the fear in our students until we see the
fear in ourselves" is one good way of looking at what happens to us when
we get caught wrestling with our "students from hell." Psychoanalysts
would describe what happened to Palmer and his student as "transference
and counter-transference," the processes by which clients project childhood views of their parents upon their therapists, and therapists then
find themselves feeling parental towards their clients.

Freud's great insight was that this transference and counter-transference
business is not a bad thing. Quite the opposite: By examining his own
reactions to a patient, an analyst can intuit how the patient's parent had
treated him as a child, or rather, how the patient had experienced that
treatment. So, the psychoanalytic view of Palmer's story might be that
when the Student from Hell sat huddled at the back of the class as if he
were facing his alcoholic father, Palmer found himself as enraged as the
father this Student felt oppressed by. But whatever way one interprets
the situation, the essential fact is that a teacher's own reaction to a difficult student contains useful information if the teacher can free himself for
a moment from that reaction to perceive what is happening to him.

Who is writing the script?

Each teacher has his own nemesis. Students like Kato and Lila, students
who come right out and challenge what I'm doing in class, may be a

pain in the ass, but they don't push my buttons. My personal Students from Hell are the quiet, passive-aggressive ones who smile no matter what I say. The ones who, when I give them feedback like, "Can you feel that your arms have dropped out of the work?" reply with a sweet: "Oh, no, I didn't. Sorry. I'll be sure to do that next time." Or those whose reaction to, "So now we're going to do that exercise again," is just to roll their eyes and shake their heads as if to say, "Oh, great. That's just great." Those are the kind that get to me. As Christopher said about Kato: I just want to wring their necks. When that happens, if I'm lucky, I feel my blood rising and note the moment. If I can't figure out a safe way to put the energy between us to work right then, I'll try to let the moment pass, watching more carefully for another opening.

But teaching is not psychoanalysis; and in the classroom, I'm not actually thinking about transference and counter-transference. My actual experience of such moments is more one of "role playing." The student is "performing" one aspect of himself—a side of himself he's probably developed over many years. Unconsciously he's playing a "role," proposing a script of sorts, and "casting" me in the complementary part: "I'm the bratty kid, and you're the punishing parent." Or "I'm depressed, and you've got to comfort me." Or "I'm sexy, and you've got to be turned on." Or whatever.

In these situations, the most import thing to remember is that the obstacle such a student presents is not a sign that the student is out to get you. On the contrary, strange as it may seem, it is a signal that you have been "accepted" as a teacher. It is an invitation to join a game, to perform your role in a script that is playing, unconsciously, in the student's mind. It is a sign that the student is willing to display his most difficult habits to you, so, even when those habits include "I hate teachers," it is a challenge the teacher must do his best to accept. It is an improvisation, and as with all improvisations, the basic rule is: You must begin by saying, "Yes." Only after accepting the invitation can you begin to rewrite the script.

When I'm on my game, what I'm doing at such moments is, first of all, letting the student know: I see what is going on and I'm not ignoring the game. And then, once we're both in the game, I'm working to change the script from the inside, helping the student see that it is possible to play with these volatile "negative energies" without staying forever stuck in the one role he keeps enacting, helping him discover that he can make new, creative choices out of the violent or depressive or sexy energy that seems to have him in its grip.

In my classes, I often join the students during their group warm-up, and if during that time I sense a student is acting out such a game, I will stay open to the student's process while I attempt to enlarge the playing field. Perhaps I will begin by responding to a student's bratty behavior by acting bratty in return, getting in his way as he runs around the room. The student picks up his cue, starting to play-fight with me: "Really?" he seems to be saying, "You mean it's okay that I'm acting this way?"

I start to rush at him, but then I switch to slow motion, and maybe I'll (slowly) say, "Come on, let's fight, but please, slow motion, okay?" The moment the student joins in the slow motion battle with me, he is wordlessly acknowledging that he can, indeed, work with his aggression in a more controlled way. But it is only by first accepting the student's bratty game that I gain enough credence to alter the rules.

Perhaps another student is curled up in the corner as if to say: "I'm very depressed. I deserve your pity. Look, at me, I'm curled up, whimpering here on the floor." Should I put my arm on her shoulder? I decide not to. I want her to know I perceive what's happening for her, but I also want to offer her a way out. Rather than offering a comforting touch, perhaps I try to compress her body even more as if to say: "Okay, but I'll bet you could act even more depressed than that. How about this?"

After a moment she starts pushing back against me, expressing the emotion beneath the depression: "What are you doing? I don't need to curl up that tightly. I'm not *that* depressed." Then, suddenly, she breaks free and suddenly starts running around the room. She's learning that her depressive pose is a role that actually contains many other emotions, emotions she's hidden—from others and from herself—but which are now bubbling to the surface. She is learning these things with her whole body, not as a therapeutic remedy for a psychological disorder, but as a new, creative resource.

As a teacher of physical acting, these are the kinds of games that work for me, but each teacher must discover his or her own way of returning the "transference" ball his student has served. Since emotions are the very notes an actor must learn to play, each of these strategies aims at helping students discover that the emotion they are experiencing at the moment, the anger they are feeling toward the teacher for instance, is an energy they can acknowledge and play with, not just a habit within which they are trapped.

In other disciplines, such as dance or music, teachers may find the transference material showing up in less obvious forms. A music student might express his anger by over-rehearsing a piece, unaware that he is undermining himself by reifying his performance until it is perfect—and dead. A dancer might keep missing the same entrance, thus obtaining the attention of the teacher she unconsciously craves. And if the teacher becomes caught and suddenly shouts at the student, then the student can break into tears, having confirmed with the teacher's complicity her own negative opinion of herself. To work effectively with such habits, each teacher, once she is aware of how these games work upon her, must find a strategy that accepts the offered bait without becoming caught on the hidden hook. I don't know what will work for you, but I do know this: There are two strategies that will *not* work.

The first strategy that will not work is to ignore the game entirely. Whatever else is going on in these encounters, the student is saying, "notice me." The fact is, you *have* noticed him, maybe more than noticed. To pretend you haven't is both a rejection and a lie. This student is sending energy your way, "reaching out" to you in his strange fashion, so if you can figure out how to play the hand he has dealt you, this could be a "teachable moment." Resistance is actually an offer to work. It becomes a "problem" when we see it as one.

The second unworkable strategy is to simply play the role in which you've been cast. That's what happened with Christopher and Kato. As soon as Christopher told him to "take off those goddamned boots," he was speaking lines that Kato was writing for him. That's what almost happened to me with the "depressed" student. If I'd put my arm around her shoulder, I'd be confirming her self-image as someone in need of pity. She needed to know I was there, and that I was aware of what she was going through. But she didn't need me to encourage her in a habit that undermined her capacity to work.

Over time, I've learned a thing or two about how to handle difficult students—or rather how to handle myself when working with them. But the principal lesson I have learned is that I still have more to learn.

When nothing seems to work

Torrence was a young man who always did his warm-up at the far end of the room near the wall; in fact, throughout each class period he spent as much time as he could near that wall. It clearly provided something for him, but it was also severely restricting his range of movement and his ability to interact with the others in the class.

I tried pointing his habit out to him, I tried cajoling him to take excursions into other areas, and I tried leaving him alone. But no matter which tactic I tried, it seemed to have no effect. So after class one day I asked Torrence to come talk to me.

"How's the work going?"

"Fine."

"Do you notice that you are still moving along the wall and avoiding the center of the room?"

"No."

"When I point it out, does it seem true?"

"What am I supposed to find in the center of the room?"

"I don't know."

"Then why would I go there?"

"Because you can't know unless you try."

"That's not a very good reason."

"It's your choice."

"Yes."

I was stumped. I could feel how uncomfortable he was, but the conversation we had made it clear that he wasn't willing to engage with me. Unlike the student who says, "Why are we doing these exercises?" Torrence did not confront me or admit that anything was wrong. His attitude towards me was beyond "passive-aggressive," and I couldn't find the way to "join the game" he was playing. I couldn't even decipher the rules. It just seemed to me as if he was avoiding the work—and me—by staying up against that wall. It was as if he felt like the wall was between us, as if we were not actually in the same room at all. During the ensuing weeks I alternated between feeling enormously frustrated and complimenting myself for not getting angry with him. I comforted myself by remembering the comment James Zull quotes from one frustrated teacher he interviewed:

> You can teach well, do all the right things, without any learning. Learning is up to the student. If I am teaching right, I am doing my part.
> (Zull, 2002, p. 19)

With Torrence, it seemed to me, I'd done everything I knew how to do. I knew it wasn't going to be helpful for me to blame Torrence for his resistance or blame myself for Torrence's failure to learn. Maybe, I thought, some other year he'll find a teacher he can trust.

What I didn't acknowledge was that in a way there *was* a wall between us, and that, from Torrence's point of view, we actually *were* not in the same room: since both of us could see—but neither dared mention—that I was white and straight, and he was gay and black.

Chapter 8

Cultures of oppression and resistance

Even when we avoid talking about race, we are talking about race; that is, even in our avoidance of the subject, we are engaging it.

Gloria Ladson-Billings

There is a lot of silence about race in White communities, and as a consequence Whites tend to think of racial identity as something that other people have, not something that is salient for them.

Beverly Daniel Tatum

For years, I've thought of myself as a pretty sensitive teacher, but I'm also aware that, at times, I've failed to perceive what some students, especially students of color, have needed, and I've often stumbled when trying to provide a safe space for them.

Early in my teaching career, I had a strong-willed black actress as a student in my class. She had a great stage presence, but she always seemed a bit tough. I thought it might be a useful stretch for her to play someone sensitive, perhaps a love scene? So I suggested Juliet. I thought she'd take the suggestion as a compliment: a Shakespeare scene, after all. She didn't.

"Why?" she asked. "Don't you think African American plays are any good?"

Her comment woke me up to the fact that I didn't actually know many African American plays—or Asian or Latino ones for that matter—and that I had some reading to do. But then, the following year, though I had expanded my scene repertoire a bit, I discovered that adding culturally diverse choices didn't necessarily solve my problem. This time, when I suggested an African American role to another black woman, she accused me of typecasting her.

The result of such encounters was that I began to feel culturally inept, not knowing how to raise the topic of race, ethnicity, or sexual orientation in my classes. As a result, too often I allowed my own embarrassment and lack of comfort to make me wary of raising the subject at all, waiting instead for students to bring up these kinds of topics, without considering that my reticence might place an additional burden upon them.

In an effort to understand what I should do, I recently contacted an ex-student of mine, an African American actress who has often found herself the only, or one of very few, black students in classes of white students taught by white teachers. She wrote back to say that in her experience, race is frequently the "elephant in the room"; a subject everyone knows is present, but no one mentions. She added that it was very helpful to her when, in a private meeting, one of her white teachers acknowledged "the difficulty that I must experience being in such a homogeneous environment." She wrote that it had meant a great deal to her that the teacher had admitted that "this [race issue] is a thing." So I'm starting to realize that, as the teacher, I must not allow my own discomfort to become an excuse for me to leave it to the minority students in my class to raise whatever issues they may have.

So, just what are "the issues?" Well, of course they are different for every student. For some, the issues they feel may have to do with things such as skin-color, hair, or clothing, but for others it may be more about personal space, about language, socio-economic class, or cultural mores. Each student may feel his or her minority status in a different way, but several hundred years of slavery and discrimination have made growing up black in America particularly problematic, a condition Chester Pierce describes as the daily stress of a "mundane extreme environment" (Pierce, 1975).

"Not-learning"

The stresses that minority students feel can add an extra layer of difficulty to the normal identity problems that many students face. In 1950, psychologist Eric Erikson coined the term "identity crisis" to describe the struggle most adolescents go through as they try to figure out who they are as sexual beings and as members of the society in which they live. On top of this more-or-less universal developmental task, many arts students in America find they need to justify their life choices to their families—and to themselves. They are acutely aware that to aim at a career as a performer means years of battling the odds economically. If the student comes from a working-class background, these economic realities often weigh very heavily. In the undergraduate department at NYU, it was not uncommon to hear a student say that her parents have told her that they will allow her to study acting only if she simultaneously studies business or prepares for some other "sensible" profession.

If, on top of all this, the student is also from a minority group, if he is gay, or Latino, or black (or perhaps all-of-the-above), the identity crisis he may be coping with can be much larger than the one facing many of his classmates.

Although attitudes towards race have certainly changed during the past 50 years, African Americans in particular still grow up in a world that constantly confronts them with their otherness, surrounding them with images of appearance, of culture, and of life-style that don't match what they see in the mirror. For many black students, this isolation is exacerbated by the fact that they can find themselves the only—or almost the only—student of color in a classroom, a "token" among white students and taught by a white teacher who, no matter how sensitive and sympathetic he is, may be clueless about their inner experience. As Jean Dresden Grambs has written, "Some blacks today say that no white person can ever be astute enough to assess accurately the black experience" (Grambs, 1972, p. 174).

One terrible paradox for some black students is that they may feel that *not* to resist the teacher—any teacher, but especially a white teacher— is taboo. Fordham and Ogbu put it this way: "To behave in the manner defined as falling within a white cultural frame of reference is to 'act white' and is negatively sanctioned" (Fordham and Ogbu, 1986, p. 181). Herbert Kohl calls the kind of resistance such students engage in "not-learning," and he suggests that for some students, "not-learning" is an important coping mechanism:

> Learning how to not-learn is an intellectual and social challenge; sometimes you have to work very hard at it. It consists of an active, often ingenious, willful rejection of even the most compassionate and well-designed teaching. It subverts attempts at remediation as much as it rejects learning in the first place. It was through insight into my own not-learning that I began to understand the inner world of students who chose to not-learn what I wanted to teach. Over the years I've come to side with them in their refusal to be molded by a hostile society and have come to look upon not-learning as positive and healthy in many situations.
>
> (Kohl, 1994, p. 2)

Many of the "not-learners" with whom Kohl has worked have been black, Latino, and/or impoverished students, students who have devised these styles of resistance as a defense against an education system that often does not treat them as equals. Kohl suggests that these students sometimes cling to this defense even when they are aware that "not-learning" is interfering with their concurrent desire to succeed in class.

If a student feels—rightly or wrongly—that the only alternative to "not-learning" is accepting the society's opinion that he is deficient in one way or another, then being "resistant" in this way may actually be a sign of health and strength for him. But for the teacher faced with this not-learning style, the situation can be paradoxical. In order to support the student's struggle for self-respect, the teacher may need to forego his own desire to get the student to learn. With my student, Torrence, it never occurred to me that his very stubbornness, his apparent surliness in ignoring my suggestions, might actually have been a sign that he was working on exactly what he needed to be working on at that moment: becoming his "own man" in a straight, white man's world. I wonder if it might have helped if I had simply said something like, "I see you. And I hope you can just take something useful from what I'm offering here." I'll never know.

Making the attempt

Glenn Singleton and Curtis Linton point out that "Addressing the impact of race in education is not a 'feel good' experience. Nor is it an attempt to make White educators feel guilty, promote pity for people of color, or extract revenge on their behalf" (Singleton and Linton, 2006, p. 39). In fact, guilt-tripping can prove to be just another mechanism to avoid the discomfort of what needs to be said and heard. In her book *When Race Breaks Out,* Helen Fox describes several situations in which racial insensitivity undermines trust, but she also points out that "Political correctness is a kind of emotional manipulation that people indulge in when they don't have the courage to face differences of opinion and point of view" (Fox, 2001, p. 33).

Beverly Daniel Tatum, author of *"Why Are All the Black Kids Sitting Together in the Cafeteria?" and Other Conversations About Race,* acknowledges that raising questions of race in the classroom can be problematic, and she admits that doing so may not actually assuage the underlying problem. But, she opines, it is better than the alternative:

> How can I make the experience of my Latino, Asian, and Native students visible without tokenizing them? I am not sure that I can, but I have learned in teaching about racism that a sincere, though imperfect, attempt to interrupt the oppression of others is usually better than no attempt at all.
>
> (Tatum, 1997, p. 132)

There is, of course, a limit to how much time and energy a class can spend on any issue outside the curriculum, and there is the risk that other students in the class may resent the time spent on social or political issues that seem to be "not what we took this course to study." Yet, issues like race, gender, or sexual orientation can sometimes have such a deep, disturbing effect upon the group dynamics, that it's often worth at least opening the subject or inviting a group training specialist in to lead a class discussion. The time "wasted" in such an outside-the-curriculum discussion can help a group of students work together so much better and delve so much more deeply into their art that, in the end, it can seem that actually time has been saved.

For me as a teacher to feel safe enough to broach such issues, I must be able to perceive that it is not *me* a student is resisting but rather *something I represents to him*. But this can be difficult. Even harder can be the realization that, in the face of the "mundane extreme environmental stress" a particular student may have experienced during his life, my best efforts may not be sufficient to enable him to fully free himself from the discomfort he experiences in my class.

A few years ago, I again had a black actress in my class who seemed to be resisting at every turn what I had to say to her. When I gave her some feedback during warm-ups, she angrily accused me of picking on her. The following week, when I just let her work on her own for several days, she complained that I wasn't paying her any attention. Then, when I gave her suggestions after a scene-showing, she said that I just didn't understand what she'd been working on. Stumped and desperate, I was determined to do better than I had with Torrence, so I said to her, "Something is going wrong here between us. Is there another teacher in the studio you and I could meet with to help us with this?" She named a female teacher whom she trusted, and the three of us met together for half-an-hour.

The bottom line, she made clear, was that I was white and I was a man and so I was just not someone whose criticism she could trust. There was nothing I could do. I found myself thinking, "There has got to be something I can say here to be helpful." (Or perhaps what I was really thinking was, "There has got to be something I can do to get this person to like me and trust me.") But that was *my* problem. What mattered to her was that in that meeting she had the space to say what she needed to say. In the following weeks, her discomfort with me had lessened enough that, if I was careful to begin my feedback to her by clearly naming the many things in a scene that she was doing *right* (and that was not hard, for she was a terrific actress), then it was possible for her to accept my suggestions for further work. But she and I were never going to be really comfortable together. Her distrust of white teachers may have been based upon bitter personal experience, but she never said.

For my part, I would just have to live with the feeling that she didn't really like me, and, sad as that might be for me, the important thing was that in spite of her distrust, it was now possible for her to learn things in my class. After all, she was paying me to be her teacher, not her friend.

Internalized oppression

While some students may actively battle against the oppression they feel, others present teachers with the opposite problem, having thoroughly internalized the negative images our world has projected on them. In *The Pedagogy of the Oppressed*, Paulo Freire writes this about his illiterate students in Brazil:

> Self-depreciation is another characteristic of the oppressed, which derives from their internalization of the opinion the oppressors hold of them. So often do they hear that they are good for nothing, know nothing, and are incapable of learning anything—that they are sick, lazy, and unproductive—that in the end they become convinced of their own unfitness. ... Not infrequently, peasants in educational projects begin to discuss a generative theme in a lively manner, then stop suddenly and say to the educator: "Excuse us, we ought to keep quiet and let you talk. You are the one who knows, we don't know anything." They often insist that there is no difference between them and the animals; when they do admit a difference, it favors the animals. "They are freer than we are."
>
> (Freire, 1970, p. 45)

The students we encounter in our classes would probably never say they feel more oppressed than animals, but a few years ago, I received a call from an ex-grad student of mine that reminded me of Freire's description. Eliza phoned to ask for advice since she was having a hard time with some of her students. "What," she wanted to know, "do you do about self-destructive resistance?"

"Who are your students?" I asked.

"This is a remedial program for kids who've been difficult in school, you know. And most of them have never taken a theater class before."

"And what are they doing?"

"Whenever I ask them to get out of their seats to do a theater exercise they say things like, 'Hey, we ain't actors, you know. We the dummies.' What should I do?"

"What do *they* want to do?" I asked.

"I think all they want to do is complain."

"Hmm," I said, wondering what I would do with such a class, "Maybe you'll have to just let them complain."

"Hey, I'm not a therapist. These students already have a therapist. I'm supposed to be teaching them acting."

"Now *you're* complaining," I said.

"Sorry."

"No. I don't mean that. I mean complaining isn't necessarily a bad thing. Tell me what happens after they say, 'We the dummies'"?

"Oh, a few of them laugh. They all kind of squirm in their seats, and little by little they get up. Then some smart aleck might imitate me, you know, 'Oooh, now let's all play a game.'"

"So, what just happened?" I asked Eliza.

"When? What do you mean?"

"I mean just now on the phone, you were complaining, and I asked you to describe the complaint in more detail, and you came up with some dialogue."

"Yeah?"

"Well, maybe the complaining itself is playable."

"Hmmm," she said, "okay, I understand. I'm doubtful, but I can give it a try."

At her next class, Eliza dropped the curriculum she'd planned, and simply asked the students to tell her the worst stories they could remember about school. They had plenty to say on the subject, enough to create several scenes, and enough to build a relationship with a teacher who did not treat them as "the dummies."

The dance teacher, Eric, the man who declared that his students were "resistant," had asked, "Why are they doing this to me?" But the essence of what Freire tells us is that "resistance" is not something a student is doing *to us*. It is a reaction to something the student feels—perhaps quite rightly—has been done *to him*. Some students who push back against our teaching are doing so for idiosyncratic, personal reasons; some are resisting for reasons that have less to do with who we are as teachers than with whom we represent to them. But whatever the reason for their resistance, our job is still to teach: to teach this particular student, not to react to his projections, but rather to support his attempts to leave his fears behind. Does this mean it is our job to help our students free themselves from all the individual and historical traumas that may underlie their resistances? Are we on the line today to do battle with the many injuries our students have experienced in the past? Well, sure. As rabbi Hillel (almost) said: If not we, who? If not now, when?

****

Let's pause a moment, now, to recapitulate. In the past few chapters we've been analyzing what it is that makes some students so hard to teach, leaving us frustrated, angry, flummoxed, or just stumped. We've been examining some pathways out of this morass. But now, it seems to me, there is one more corner of this swamp that calls for our attention. The other side of transference: Falling in love.

Chapter 9

Eros et charitas

We see theatre—especially in its palpable, carnal aspect—as a place of provocation, a [place where] we are able, without hiding anything, to entrust ourselves to something we cannot name but in which live Eros and Charitas.

Jerzy Grotowski

Erotic tension between a director and an actor can be an indispensible contribution to a good rehearsal process.

Anne Bogart

For many years before writing *Angela's Ashes*, Frank McCourt made his living teaching English in New York City public high schools. In his second book, *Teacher Man,* McCourt describes the day, early in his teaching career, when he led his students at the McKee Vocational and Technical High School on Staten Island in a discussion of war poetry. He recounts how he encouraged his class to talk about soldiers they themselves knew who had returned injured from the Korean War, and he describes how well discussion was going until

> One girl with a lovely figure and wearing a lacy pink blouse said her sister was married to a guy who was wounded at Pyongyang and he had no arms at all, not even stubs where you could stick on the false arms. So her sister had to feed him and shave him and do everything and all he ever wanted was sex. Sex, sex, sex, that's all he ever wanted, and her sister was getting all worn out.

Then McCourt adds:

> I admired Helen so much for her maturity and her courage and her lovely breasts I could hardly go on with the lesson. I thought I wouldn't mind being an amputee myself if I had her near me all

day, swabbing me, drying me, giving me the daily massage. Of course teachers were not supposed to think like that but what are you to do when you're twenty-seven and someone like Helen is sitting there in front of you bringing up topics like sex and looking the way she did?

(McCourt, 2005, pp. 52–53)

McCourt is right. Teachers are *not* supposed to think like that—but they do, and not just the ones who are proud of being male, randy, and Irish. In her delightfully personal and deeply wise book, *A Life in School, What the Teacher Learned*, Jane Tompkins tells the story this way:

Sometimes the feelings I have toward my students are romantic. It's like being in love. You know how when you're in love or have a crush on somebody, you're always looking forward to the next meeting with desire and trepidation—will he or she be glad to see me? Will he or she be late? not come at all? Will she or he think I'm smart? good-looking? a nice person? It's the roller-coaster of love—up one day and down the next—no two classes the same. How soon will we be going steady? Will our love be true? Do you love me like I love you?

Tompkins ends her confession by asking:

Am I the only person who feels this way about teaching?

(Tompkins, 1996, pp. 144–45)

Of course she's not. But how should she know? For both McCourt and Tompkins (in their strikingly gender-appropriate ways) are opening the door to a room that most of us keep locked, a chamber of private thoughts and embarrassing emotions that most teachers have a hard time openly discussing with each other. As I wrote in the Introduction, when I began to teach, being infatuated with a student was not something I was prepared for, and certainly not something I would dare mention to others. Of course, the biggest problem with this problem is that it may not seem like a "problem" at all.

The tender trap

In the previous few chapters, I described how a teacher can become enmeshed in the coils of negative transference and counter-transference, and I made some suggestions about what a teacher might do to escape that trap. But what about *positive* transference? Is the process the same when struggling with the "tender trap?" Well, yes—and no. Yes, because any emotion you experience but do not acknowledge can undermine your ability to teach. And no, because the dangers of being infatuated are rather different from the dangers of being frustrated or enraged. After all, if you find yourself wanting to strangle a student, your anger provides a pretty strong motivation for you to remedy the situation. You might complain to other teachers or ask them if they are having similar difficulties with the student who was frustrating you. But if you find yourself having romantic or erotic fantasies about a student, you probably wouldn't complain to your colleagues or ask if they were also having similar fantasies, and if you're enjoying your daydreams, why look for a "remedy?"

As the writings of Tompkins and McCourt reveal, teachers of English literature are as liable to fall for their students as anyone else. In the performance disciplines, however, the problem is compounded by the fact that one of the things our students are learning from us is how to sparkle on stage with exciting and attractive energies. In other words, they are studying how to become adept at seducing their audiences. And for the moment, their audience is us. So it will not work for the teacher of a performing art simply to avoid the issue by discouraging those energies. To do so would be to undermine one of the very skills we're encouraging them to develop.

And yet ... and yet ... the dangers are real.

When I was hired to teach at Emerson College, I was informed by one of my new colleagues that the acting teacher I'd been hired to replace had, for many years, been well liked and respected by his students for his kind, gentle, and effective teaching, but that during the last couple of years, his students had found him distant and unapproachable. The back-story, I was told, was that in the course of teaching his classes, this teacher had touched some of his students, and that one of them had taken offence at this physical contact. As a consequence, the school administration had put the teacher—and the student who had brought the charges—through a long inquiry process at the end of which it was determined that the teacher had not, in fact, acted inappropriately. But by then, this teacher had become so afraid of offending his students that he had taken to not showing them any affection at all. Not only did he keep his physical distance, but he rarely smiled or made eye contact with them. As a consequence, his students, who were entirely unaware of the history, felt continually put off. After a couple of years of mutual uneasiness, he had decided to leave.

So there you have it: you're damned if you do, and you're damned if you don't. So what is a teacher to do?

A convertible currency

As an acting teacher, I'm always reminding my students that emotional energy is neither "good" nor "bad"; it is just energy. Most of the students are aware that one of their tasks as an actor will be to play with their emotions, but many of them believe that each of their emotions is separate from the others: laughter, for instance, is entirely different from—and incompatible with—tears. But during our work together they learn that, actually, they can slide from genuine laughter to real tears and back again by simply changing their vocal placement and pitch. They begin to understand that feelings—their own, real feelings—are not solid, immutable substances, but fluid, malleable energies. In particular, as I pointed out earlier, they learn that the one emotion they think of as the most "illegal"—fear—is not just a hindrance to be hidden or denied, but a wonderful source of energy on stage—if they permit themselves to acknowledge and inhabit its power. Since stage fright is such a common problem for performers, I imagine that this particular lesson is one that most teachers of performance are quite used to imparting.

But it may be much more difficult for a teacher to recognize that what is true for performers is just as true for teachers. That *all* the emotions we feel toward our students—the fear, the frustration, the anger, and even the emotions we think of as the most "illegal"—infatuation and desire—are energies we can actually convert into helpful teaching tools, if we are willing to acknowledge and work with them. It's a lesson I've struggled to learn many times in my own teaching—with more and with less success.

A few years ago, a tall blonde student with soulful, dark brown eyes told me as she entered my workshop that, after reading my book, she'd saved her money for two years just to be able to study with me. She explained that she'd become disheartened with always being cast to play the sexy parts in musical comedies, and that she'd come to my workshop hoping to be pushed beyond what she knew. I was flattered.

After many of our exercises, this young actress would smile and enthuse about the work. Although sometimes I found her eagerness cloying, there was something about that smile, and the way she moved. She clearly liked me, and wanted very badly for me to like her, and perhaps she was unaware of the energy she radiated—or of the effect it had. Her transference seemed quite evident. My counter-transference was less obvious—to me.

All through that workshop, I thought I was trying my best to push her beyond the slow, gentle acting habits she'd developed over years. When we got to scene-work, I suggested that she stretch her repertoire by playing Amanda, the cruel mother in *Glass Menagerie*. When she did, she managed to portray a rather nasty Amanda, but perhaps I should have noticed as I was coaching her, that she seemed to bring much more energy to the more sensual section of the scene, in which Amanda remembers her own alluring youth, than she did to those moments when Amanda mistreats her daughter.

In retrospect, I think this student's acting work became deeper during those three weeks—but not very much. I remember suspecting that beneath the sweet enthusiasm she always showed the world, there lay a layer of other emotions—bitterness perhaps? or distain? or despair?—that she never revealed. Whatever that layer was, I don't think I helped her uncover it. Afterwards I began to wonder: Did I let her get away with her habits because I was caught in the web of her flattery and her fetching looks? Did I fear that if I disturbed the genteel self-image she projected, or challenged the winning smiles she shot my way, she might have reacted by knocking me off the pedestal on which she had placed me or by showering me with some of that underlying bitterness and distain?

With other students, I think I've done a better job. I remember another young woman in one of my acting classes who came to class every day wearing a tight leotard with a plunging neckline, and who seemed always to be flirting—with me and with everyone else—while she did her warm ups. Her eyes were always seeking contact with other eyes, and, like a classical musician who is so good at keeping time that he can't swing a tune with syncopation, her body seemed caught in one rather sensual rhythm, no matter what gestures or emotions another student cast her way.

I didn't know how to address the problem verbally. I didn't think it would help to just say, "You've got to stop being so sexy." So, at a loss for words, I simply stepped into the group warm up and worked by turns with many of the students, responding to the energy they put out, and then changing it, sometimes following, sometimes leading, always hinting at rhythms and emotions that might extend their particular physical, vocal, and emotional vocabularies. When I reached this particular student, she immediately approached me with her come-hither gaze, her hips sashaying left and right, her arms outstretched. For a moment I allowed myself to reflect the energy she was emanating, as if to say, "Yes, indeed, you're sexy … and that's okay." For me, that moment was both delightful and uncomfortable, because the delight was awfully easy to get lost in. But the very danger of that delight then served me as an acting source; my fear of getting lost in the allure, motivated me to pull away from her and suddenly fall to the floor. When she saw me crouched there, enacting my dread of being caught in her web, her sexual energy began to drain. Her habitual smile relaxed, and suddenly she stopped moving. Dropping her sensual vocabulary entirely, she bent down, reached out and simply asked, "Are you okay?"

As she did, her gesture and the tone of her voice were entirely new. For the first time in the warm up she was not "performing" an emotion. Now perhaps, I could help her sense that other emotions, like the "real" concern she was showing me, were no less performative than the sexy forms she was so used to. Starting to move again, I fixed my gaze on frightful images I envisioned standing directly behind her. Suddenly she turned as if she too could sense the phantoms in that empty space. By turning to stare towards that vacancy, she not only released herself from her habitual, sexy acting patterns, but, since she was no long facing towards me, she also freed herself from the interpersonal energy upon which she usually depended. Free of that fix, her imagination could take her into new realms, and what began as a shudder of fear suddenly transformed into a sneering vehemence as she confronted the images she herself had conjured, and she plunged into uncharted waters.

At the end of that warm up I was able to say to her, "So, it seems there are more flavors of reality available for you to play with," thus encouraging new discoveries, rather than simply discouraging her old habits. For her, I think, this lesson was a valuable first step towards a richer acting vocabulary. For me, the lesson was that there was nothing immoral in my impulse to respond to flirtation by flirting back, for having once accepted the invitation to share erotic energies, I could help this student move beyond her habits into new and uncharted realms.

So, the sexual energy a teacher may experience while working with a student is not "wrong," any more than the anger we may feel toward our Students from Hell is "wrong." Positive transference, like the negative kind, is a signal, an invitation to engage, and it offers an indication of exactly what "language" will allow a particular student to feel heard. To stifle our reactions to that energy is tantamount to telling the student, "You shouldn't be exuding such sexual energy. There's something wrong with you," and it may be experienced as such.

Feminist author bell hooks tells this apposite story:

> During my first semester of college teaching, there was a male student in my class whom I always seemed to see and not see at the same time. At one point in the middle of the semester, I received a call from a school therapist who wanted to speak with me about the way I treated this student in the class. The therapist told me that the student had said I was unusually gruff, rude, and downright mean when I related to him. I did not know exactly who the student was,

could not put a face or body with his name, but later when he identified himself in class, I realized that I was erotically drawn to this student. And that my naive way of coping with feelings in the classroom that I had been taught never to have was to deflect (hence my harsh treatment of him), repress, and deny.

(hooks, 1994, p. 192)

Touch

As an acting teacher, part of my job is to encourage my students to feel and to display their emotions—all their emotions—without judgment. I can't do that while attempting to deny my own. In order to teach I must let myself feel everything I am feeling—as long as I can remain conscious of my reactions and am able to put the energy I'm experiencing to pedagogical use. Often enough, in my physical acting work, that means allowing myself to touch a student, in spite of the dangers the Emerson teacher I mentioned encountered.

When I began to teach, I often hesitated, afraid that touching a student was a violation of the correct pedagogical distance. I did not trust myself—perhaps rightly so—for at that time I was, indeed, apt to become quickly and unconsciously frustrated by—or infatuated with—my students.

But with time, I've learned to trust—and to monitor—my pedagogical impulses. When, during an actor's warm-up, I see a student gesturing fully with her arms, hands, and face, but then walking mechanically and unexpressively to another location in the room, I will suspect that she is blocking some of the energy in her legs and pelvis. Often I will ask such a student to sit down on the floor opposite me and place the soles of her feet against mine, and then I'll encourage her to push me with her feet across the room. Suddenly all the energy in her lower body has an outlet, and the power with which she drives me across the floor can feel simultaneously violent and sexual. This kind of physical contact provides a safe form that can allow a student to discover that the both these energies, the violent and the sexual, are real—and workable.

Similarly, if I see an actor presenting an angry monologue in a disconnected, intellectual way, I may grab hold of his leg, and then let him drag me around the room while reciting his text. Or, if I notice that a student keeps lowering his eyes or whispering as he speaks, I may place my hand in the middle of his back, letting his body sense that it is safe to enter fully into the emotion that is rising within him.

This past year, a visitor to my Shakespeare monologue class observed me working with two students as they performed their monologues. The first was a man who was working on King Lear's "Reason not the need ... " speech. As he performed, this powerful actor kept hunching his shoulders forward and pumping up his anger, even on lines like:

> You see me here, you gods, a poor old man,
> As full of grief as age, wretched in both.
>
> (*King Lear*, Act II, Scene 4)

At first I simply urged him to try working on his knees, lifting his eyes, his hands and his voice to heaven, but still his back remained tense, and so did his voice. So then, as he started his monologue once more, I knelt behind him and coached him to relax his weight back upon me. As he allowed me to carry his weight, his voice began to crack, and suddenly Lear's lines:

> You think I'll weep.
> No, I'll not weep.
> I have full cause of weeping, but this heart
> Shall break into a hundred thousand flaws,
> Or ere I'll weep.

resonated with deep meaning. My back had provided a kind of support and safety my words could not.

The second student I worked with that day was a woman who was performing a speech of Constance, in *King John*, a speech in which the character imagines her captive son is already dead. But as she spoke the lines:

> Grief fills the room up of my absent child,
> Lies in his bed, walks up and down with me ...
>
> (*King John*, Act III, Scene 4)

she averted her eyes and lowered her voice, subtly avoiding the enormity of Constance's despair. I asked this student to go through the speech once more, very slowly, taking care to breathe, and as she did, I sat down beside her, placing my open palm in the middle of her back. This time all her words vibrated, her whole body shook, and as she spoke, tears rolled down her cheeks.

After the class, the visitor caught me in the hallway and asked, "How do you know how to touch your students? It looks almost like magic."

"I don't know," I replied, "It's often a mystery to me in the moment. But I've learned to trust my impulse. And then, if I'm wrong, I can sense that pretty quickly and try something else." Perhaps I should also have pointed out to this visitor that the "magic" she thought she'd witnessed depended upon the weeks of physical sensitivity these students had developed, and that actually, the best conjuring trick was when the students ran through their speeches one more time without the touch. For it was in those subsequent run-throughs that they discovered they could give themselves the support they needed on their own. The lesson, after all, is never complete until the performer knows that she's in charge of her own magic.

Nota Bene: For learning to happen, a student must trust her teacher, and that trust must be earned. But what earns a student's trust depends a great deal on the particular student's history—history the teacher may not know. I have become aware that students who come to performance training with a history of abuse may be unable to withstand even the gentlest touch. So, when I feel the impulse to touch a student, I often check first, sometimes non-verbally, sometimes with words: "I'm going to hold on to your foot now. Tell me if this is not okay."

Eros, Charitas, and power

The angry or erotic impulses a teacher may feel toward a student are not the problem: these are simply emotions that must be made conscious and put to good use. (As the Bogart quote at the top of this chapter suggests, the same holds true for a director working with a performer.) No, the real problem is that in a classroom—or in a rehearsal—these volatile energies are layered upon the power inequities inherent in the situation.

Educator Peter Elbow, a highly respected teacher of teaching, puts it this way:

> The one thing sure is that teaching is sexual. What is uncertain is which practices are natural and which are unnatural, which fruitful and which barren, which legal and which illegal. When the sexuality of teaching is more generally felt and admitted, we may finally draw the obvious moral: it is a practice that should only be performed upon the persons of consenting adults.
>
> (Elbow, 1986, p. 70)

But that, of course, is the catch. No matter what their ages or their genders, what happens between a teacher and student is never quite a practice engaged in by "consenting adults," for there is an inescapable inequity in power between teacher and student. (More on this in the next chapter.)

On the other hand, if, as Jane Tompkins put it, you "have a crush on somebody, [or] you're always looking forward to the next meeting with desire and trepidation … " it is important to remember that, even though these desires may feel uncomfortable, they are also an indication of your caring about the student. And caring is not a bad thing.

Theater, said Jerzy Grotowski, depends upon "the attitude of giving and receiving which springs from true love" (Grotowski, 1976, 81, p. 35), and that loving act, he pointed out, includes both *eros* and *charitas*. The same is true of teaching, for at bottom, good teaching is an act of love. Whether that love is expressed as a touch, a smile, or a challenge, a critical insight or a word of encouragement, what good teachers give their students is the sensation of being seen and heard and appreciated—that is, they give them the experience of being loved. bell hooks, in fact, asserts that, if they wish to inspire learning, teachers must dare to use their erotic energy:

> When eros is present in the classroom setting, then love is bound to flourish. … To restore passion to the classroom … professors must find again the place of eros within ourselves and together allow the mind and body to feel and know desire.
>
> (hooks, 1994, pp. 187, 199)

Certainly, one of the most striking moments during the 1967 workshop with Jerzy Grotowski occurred when Grotowski was working with the actor Larry Pine. For many long minutes Grotowski had encouraged Larry to let his voice travel through different body-resonators, sometimes telling him to listen with his body to the echo of his own voice, sometimes thumping him in the middle of the back saying, "*La bouche ici! La bouche ici!*" (Put your mouth, here!) After 20 minutes of this mysterious process, Larry, who was a rather tough guy, looked entirely cooked. Grotowski then sat down on the carpet in the middle of the studio, took Larry into his lap, and just cradled him there for several minutes. It was the most tender, loving, and intimate moment I've ever seen between a teacher and a student.

I think that for me, the act of offering love is what makes teaching a joyous experience. I can't imagine teaching without it. But then, allowing oneself to feel love towards one's students is only half of the difficulty. The other half is undergoing the pain of losing it.

Chapter 10

The broken heart

Ein shalem mi lev shavur. (There is nothing as whole as a broken heart.)
Rabbi Menachem Mendel of Kotzk, Poland (1787–1859)

In Tennessee Williams' play, *Camino Real*, the un-heroic hero, Kilroy, falls
in love with Esmeralda, a beautiful young Mexican woman who, in
addition to her earthly charms, possesses the magical ability to renew
her virginity at every full moon. She is, of course, irresistible. What
could be more wonderful than the ability to encounter every love—or any
other pleasure—as if for the first time? Wonderful ... and impossible.

Yet that is exactly what a performer must do, night after night: She
must begin every performance—the first steps of each dance, the first
notes of each concerto or the first scene of each play—unburdened by
her knowledge of how the music climaxes or where the story leads. If
Juliet were to "know" what happens at the end of the story, she might
think twice before falling in love with Romeo; but of course, the actress
playing Juliet *does* know. After all, she has rehearsed the tomb scene
many times.

In my acting teaching, I often remind students that an actor is constantly falling in love—with her scene partner, with her lines, with a
production—and then having to let that love go. In fact, each time one
breaks eye contact there is a twinge of sorrow to be felt. One might
even say that to stay fully alive in performance is to experience a tiny
taste of death over and over. The trick is not to shy away from that
pain nor to steel oneself against falling in love again the next night.

The Sufis call this ability to stay open in spite of our sorrows, "Living
with a Broken Heart." It is a capacity we all possess. Once upon a time,
each of us was a child who could laugh and run, and fall, and cry, and
then pick himself up from the fall and start into running and laughing
again. Many of us have been lovers who fall in love, lose that love, and
then—after a period of mourning, perhaps—allow ourselves to fall in

love all over again, just as the actress playing Juliet must do, night after night.

As teachers, our job includes the ability to endure our students' resistances, their anger, their despair, and their momentary love, without becoming hardened or protecting ourselves from the pain or the rejection we may face again later. We must allow our hearts to bleed for a moment, and then, like Esmeralda, we must open ourselves to the next Student from Hell—or Heaven—with an undiminished capacity for understanding, equanimity, and love.

I remember a young student who came to my office to talk to me week after week for most of a semester. He wasn't even in my acting class, but as my advisee, we'd established a relationship he seemed to need. For many weeks he talked about his anger at societal inequities and his overwhelming feelings of powerlessness to change the world. Sometimes he mentioned suicide. Why, he wanted to know, should he waste his life making art when both the world and he himself were in such pain? His teachers told me they thought he was a talented actor, but that his deep depressions and his violent outbursts made it hard for him to work.

Most of the time when he talked, I just listened. Over time, it seemed to me that he began to change; his mood seemed less oppressive and his teachers told me his work in classes had improved. I have no idea whether his meetings with me were instrumental in his improvement—maybe he had a good therapist outside of school, maybe he fell in love. But I do know that I worked really hard to just be there for him and to be supportive of him, no matter how gloomy his moods. By the following semester, he had become one of the most sought-after actors in the studio. He was cast in many shows, and seemed to have a glowing confidence on stage I could not have imagined from him the semester before. Then he would pass me in the hallways without a word or a look. He was free, he was doing well, his art was improving. He didn't need me anymore, and it hurt.

It was a painful lesson for me as a teacher. I wanted to be acknowledged, thanked, paid back somehow for all those hours of listening. I wanted not to feel the sorrow of having lost this love. There was, I realized, a certain irony in this, for this young man's independence, his ability to feel good about himself and his work were evidence that I had done my job well. So each time he passed me in the hallway, I experienced a mixture of satisfaction and loss, an amalgam of pride and heart-break.

Good enough teaching

Sixty years ago, the psychologist D. W. Winnicott coined the phrase, "good enough mothering" to describe the parent who could, without withdrawing or retaliating, allow her child to express whatever he was feeling, including moments of violence or anger at the parent.[1] In a similar way, "good enough teachers" must create a space in which students can express whatever they need to express as creative artists without fear that they will be punished or reprimanded for doing so. Sometimes that includes allowing ourselves as teachers to be the targets for their resistance, their aggression or their growls of "I hate you" in the midst of the work. At other times—as with my suicidal student—it means letting ourselves care deeply about a student though we may suffer later for having cared so much.

At times, being a "good enough teacher" may also mean allowing a student to reject not you but the discipline you are teaching. Several years ago, two young women in my acting class were working on the final scene from Martin McDonagh's play, *The Beauty Queen of Leenane*. It's a scene of strong emotion and of violent give-and-take, and it presents American actors with some wonderful character challenges. At the climax of the scene, the daughter, enraged at her mother for years of cruelty and for lying to her about a love-letter, punishes her by holding the mother's hand down on a hot stove. The script says the mother "screams in pain and terror" while the daughter accuses her of hiding the letter sent by the man she loves.

In my class, when the actress playing the daughter pulled the mother's hand towards the hot stove, the mother started to look towards her but quickly looked down and seemed to drop out of the scene.

"There's nothing more you need to do," I said. "Just look up at her as you did, and don't close across the chest." We tried the moment again, and for a moment the mother glanced up at the daughter and, as she did, a look of horror crossed her face, but again she quickly lowered her eyes and pulled out of the scene, collapsing onto the floor.

"What happened?" I asked.

"I ... I just don't want to do it," she said.

"You could feel what was happening there?"

"Yes. I know. I just ... don't want to do it."

---

1 Psychologist David Wallin puts it this way: "[I]t is only the child who forcefully expresses her anger and discovers that her parent 'survives destruction'—neither retaliating nor withdrawing—who has the opportunity to learn that the other is, in fact, a separate subject rather than an object" (Wallin, 2007, p. 56). In other words, the parent who retaliates gives the child the impression that it is the child's emotions and actions that control those of the parent, who is a mere extension of himself. It is only when the parent accepts the child's actions without retaliation that the child can perceive that the parent is a separate being, and it is this perception that allows the child to separate himself.

The art-making part of me thought: I should help this young woman accomplish this moment on stage. The look of horror that had crossed her face for a moment had been just right. If this young woman could be helped to let go of her need to control what she was feeling, I felt sure the terror and the tears the scene called for would emerge. Perhaps, I thought, if I had her slow the moment down or scream more forcefully as she looks at her scene partner ... and yet her "I just don't want to do it," spoke to another part of me.

"That's fine," I said. "There is no need. The important thing is that you see what the work is. But it is your choice. It's up to you."

In that moment, I wasn't sure why I'd backed off; but later I was glad I hadn't pushed, even though stopping where we did may have been frustrating for her, and certainly was for her scene partner and for the rest of the class who were anticipating the cathartic end of the scene. I was glad because the acting lesson seemed, ultimately, less important than another lesson she was learning right then: the "choice" lesson. If I had pushed her, it would have been my choice, not hers. Unlike my student Lila, who chose to join the improv warm-up after watching for a week, this young woman was choosing *not* to do the work. In this case it was a bit harder to let myself appreciate her act of choosing since what she was choosing was to walk away from the work I was trying to teach.

Perhaps a year or two later this young woman would find that she was ready to undergo the emotional exposure that acting requires. Or perhaps not. Many students discover at some point that acting is not all high-energy excitement, performance and applause, and that the kind of "work" it requires often feels uncomfortable, personal—or just not what they had thought it would be. At such moments, it is easy for a student to feel that she has "failed" as a performer—and easy for the teacher to feel that she has "failed" as a teacher. But with a little compassion for the student, it may be possible to help her see that deciding to change her professional goals is not just evidence of having "failed," but a positive decision to steer her life in another direction. With a little compassion for oneself, it may be possible for a teacher to see that she has not just "failed" at teaching a performance skill but has helped a student learn to trust herself, encouraging an ability that will serve her in many aspects of her life.

As far as I can see, you cannot teach this kind of work without offering your heart; and you cannot offer your heart while protecting it from being broken. Therefore, a teacher is liable to have her heart broken in small ways again and again. Yet, she must go on offering it, for it is the consistent beating of that heart that provides what Eloise

Ristad called the "climate" in which a student can "accept permission to be free of the usual restriction." Or more accurately, what the teacher provides is the *illusion* of creating that climate, an illusion sufficient to sustain the student until she realizes that it is *she*, not the teacher, who creates that climate for herself. Perhaps a good teacher is like the feather in the film *Dumbo:* both a magical source of power—and nothing at all.

How is a teacher to tolerate this paradoxical condition? How can she perform her role as a magical talisman knowing full well that to accomplish her magic, she must permit himself to be cast aside at the end?

Toward the end of Samuel Beckett's *Endgame*, Clov wonders aloud:

CLOV: There's one thing I'll never understand ... Why I always obey you. Can you explain that to me?
HAMM: No ... Perhaps it's compassion.
(*Pause.*)
A kind of great compassion.

(Beckett, 1958, p. 76)

Pause

In the first chapters of this book, I set out to describe the *via negativa*, a process that enables students to free themselves from the blocks to learning and creativity they have accrued since childhood. I wrote that this "road backwards" can be difficult—both for the students who travel it and for the teachers who attempt to be their guides along the path. In the chapters that followed, I have described some of the obvious hazards and the hidden pitfalls that students and teachers may encounter along the way. But perhaps while enumerating so many traps and perils, I've lost sight of the one thing that makes the whole trip worthwhile. After all, this expedition is a journey of liberation, a way of recovering the natural joys of learning and of creating with which all of us were born. So at this point I'd like to propose a short pause to remind us all of one of Grotowski's most basic lessons: The lesson about there being No Mistakes.

No mistakes

There is something in each of us that yearns for gentle, loving permission to make mistakes—to be a beloved child, loved no matter how much we goof. ... When we give ourselves the power to fail, we at the same time give ourselves the power to excel.

Eloise Ristad

For several days at the start of the 1967 workshop at NYU, Jerzy Grotowski and his leading actor, Ryszard Cieslak, instructed us in headstands of all kinds: Tripod headstands, shoulder-stands, elbow-stands, ear-stands, hand-stands. We students tilted left and right, sweated and wobbled, struggling to keep our balance until we crashed to the floor. When we did, Grotowski would say: "When you fall, ... you must think of the ground as someone or something that loves you and will not reject you" (Crawley, 1978, IV, 1).

When he would say things like that, I would think, "That sounds profound ... but I have no idea what he's talking about." What could it possibly mean to think of the ground as "something that loves you"?

Then one day some years later, as I was watching a one-year-old child stand, walk, fall, stand, fall, cry, laugh, stand, walk, and fall again, I realized that there *had* indeed been a time when the ground had "loved" me, when the floor had been my home base, always there to return to when I fell, a home that would receive me and support me until I was ready to stand again—albeit sometimes with a bump. Watching that child, I realized that when I was small I hadn't thought of the bump as an insult. It was simply an integral part of the process, not something I must be frightened of, and certainly not evidence of having failed. After all, how would any child ever learn to walk if every time he fell down, someone said to him, "No. No. You've failed. You'll never make it. Why don't you just stick with crawling?"

Yet that is exactly the lesson we start learning a little later on: If at first you don't succeed, try, try again—but don't forget: basically, you're a failure, and failure is a terrible thing, so rather than admit to failure—lie about it.

How do we learn such a terrible lesson?

In an article about the work of Carol S. Dweck, a psychology professor at Stanford University, Alina Tugend reported in *The New York Times* in 2007 that we learn it directly from our parents and our teachers:

> Studies with children and adults show that a large percentage cannot tolerate mistakes or setbacks. ... In particular, those who believe that intelligence is fixed and cannot change tend to avoid taking chances that may lead to errors.
>
> Often parents and teachers unwittingly encourage this mind-set by praising children for being smart rather than for trying hard or struggling with the process.
>
> For example, in a study that Professor Dweck and her researchers did with 400 fifth graders, half were randomly praised as being "really smart" for doing well on a test; the others were praised for their effort.
>
> Then they were given two tasks to choose from: an easy one that they would learn little from but do well, or a more challenging one that might be more interesting but induce more mistakes.
>
> The majority of those praised for being smart chose the simple task, while 90 percent of those commended for trying hard selected the more difficult one. ...
>
> They were then given another test, above their grade level, on which many performed poorly. Afterward, they were asked to write anonymously about their experience to another school and report their scores. Thirty-seven percent of those who were told they were smart lied about their scores, while only 13 percent of the other group did.
>
> "One thing I've learned is that kids are exquisitely attuned to the real message, and the real message is, 'Be smart,'" Professor Dweck said. "It's not, 'We love it when you struggle, or when you learn and make mistakes.'"
>
> (Tugend, 2007)

When you seek to avoid making mistakes, you also avoid many possibilities for "accidental" success. Sticky-notes, for instance, were invented by someone who was trying to invent a new, strong, instant-stick glue. He "failed" because, while his new glue stuck easily, it also unstuck easily. Thomas Alva Edison, famous for having invented the light bulb and the phonograph (among hundreds of other useful and not-so-useful things) is also famous for having responded to a *New York Times* reporter who asked him how it felt to have failed 700 times in his attempts to invent a better light bulb:

> I have not failed 700 times. I have not failed once. I have succeeded in proving that those 700 ways will not work. When I have eliminated the ways that will not work, I will find the way that will work.

Experimentation is the very foundation of creativity in science and in art. Unless you are like Mozart and have a direct line to God, making art of any kind is a process of trying things out, playing with them for a while and then throwing away most of what you found. Unlike Mozart, Beethoven needed to try over and over before arriving at his final melodic choices. The sketches Picasso made before painting "Guernica" are a great tribute to the joys of experimentation.

An actor on his head

Grotowski's headstand lesson is based upon the idea that when you experiment, you can't know where the experiment will lead you. If, while attempting a headstand, you start to lose your balance, then *that's* what you are now exploring: balance-losing. Once you tilt, there are two choices: one is to fight the tilt, the other is to get into the wobble. Either way, you are no longer just "doing a headstand," what you are doing is "fighting" or "wobbling." And either way, you have not "failed" at the headstand. As soon as something new starts happening, it won't do to pretend it's not, so you might as well treat is as if that was what you meant to be doing. This kind of *post hoc justification* is one of the essential secrets of all improvisation: whatever happens, treat it as though it happened on purpose. There are no mistakes—only interesting surprises.

It is appropriate that Grotowski's lesson about non-failure is grounded (as it were) in a recognition of how very important our relationship to the floor can be. On the one hand, it was the evolutionary leap of getting up off the floor into an erect, bipedal posture that allowed the genus "homo" to develop infant-tending and agriculture—not to mention ballet and skate-boarding—thus making much of human progress possible. On the other hand, becoming "upright" also resulted in our losing touch with our developmental history. As we raised our heads higher, lifted our buttocks onto chairs and shod our feet, we also lost touch with some of our ancient and earthy, animal nature.

The poet Terrance Keenan tells it this way:

> A man came to the rabbi and said, "Rabbi, it is written that once
> we could see the face of God. Why can't we do that anymore?
> What happened that men can no longer reach that high to see the
> face of God?"
>
> The rabbi was very old. He had seen it all. He closed his eyes and
> ran his fingers through his long beard.
>
> "My son, that is not it at all. Men cannot see the face of God
> because no one can stoop that low."
>
> (Keenan, 2001, p. 108)

So, a central element of the physical acting I teach involves getting out
of the vertical, rediscovering falling, rolling, and crawling, for there are
great stores of energy locked in our hips, our groins, our legs, and our
feet, energies that are difficult to access when we live in our heads, held
so high above the floor, and treat our lower bodies as no more than a
transportation system that carries our more instrumental arms, hands,
and heads from place to place. Working with kneeling and crawling and
rolling and falling encourages actors to give up some of their "heady"
(self)control, and forces them to experience the delightful riskiness of
making mistakes. Eloise Ristad, whom I have quoted so often, named
her book, *A Soprano on her Head*, because she discovered that one of her
singing students found new resonance in her voice by singing upside down.

So Grotowski's headstand exercise is simultaneously a literal lesson
in "getting out of your head" and a figurative lesson in being able to
reinterpret "failure." It encourages each student to confront (head-on)
his idea that "failure" is something bad, something to be avoided. This
can be a real struggle, for many of us are well schooled in trying to get
things "right" and out of touch with the joy we once knew in getting
things wrong—or rather the joy in not distinguishing between right and
wrong, the joy of simply converting each impulse, each wobble, and each
"mistake" into usable energy.

Fears of failure

American actors sometimes complain that Grotowski's lessons are hard to
do. Many attribute the difficulty to the pure physical exertion involved:
after all, why should one struggle to do "impossible" headstands when
one might just as well learn to act sitting in a chair? But actually, I don't
think it is the physical challenge that makes this work so daunting. What
makes the work hard is its endless ambiguity, its refusal to condone the

ideas of success and failure, of winning and losing that are so deeply embedded in our culture. It goes against what Max Weber called, "The Protestant Ethic and the Spirit of Capitalism," the Calvinist—and capitalist—idea that "success" is a sign of being "saved," while "failure" implies a calamity far more profound than the embarrassment of our immediate error. Failure is an indication that we are damned—forever.

As I've noticed in myself, we teachers can get caught up in these fears of failure too.

One day just recently, I had begun my acting class with an open warm-up. I encouraged people to use any of the exercises we'd studied—the Cat, the headstands, and the *plastiques*—but, I said, today we will try doing all the work without vocalizing. I said that if anyone felt a need to make sound, he should try to put the impulse into his body or make the sound "silently" by breathing out with an open throat. By the middle of the exercise, two of the students were clearly experiencing some strong energies. Their bodies were fully engaged, their faces were very alive, and they both continued the work for several minutes after the rest of the class had finished. Suddenly, one of the two began to roar. Over and over, he bellowed. It was very animalistic and very loud, but each of his roars was slightly different from the last, as if the actor were playing with the pitch of his howl, trying to make the sound capture exactly what he was experiencing. When he started to vocalize, I almost interrupted to remind him of the rule of silence I had established, but then the precision of his howling made me feel that this explosion of his was somehow "necessary," so I said nothing.

After everyone had finished, I gathered the group to share whatever they had to say about the work. When the roaring actor spoke, he explained that as soon as he had started to make sound, he had realized that he was breaking the rules and immediately anticipated that the teacher would quiet him, but that this thought itself had angered him even further and made him want to roar all the louder. It was a neat description of exactly how rule-breaking works, so after he'd spoken, I talked to the whole group about the necessity of sometimes breaking the rules.

"There are moments," I said, "When you have done everything you can do inside the form you started with. And at such moments, you must go beyond the form."

The other student whose work had been so energetic gave me a startled look, but she said nothing. At the end of the class, however, as I was about to walk out the door, she came up to me and said she wanted to talk. As soon as the office door closed behind us, she burst out.

"Why did you do that?"

"Do what?"

"Change the rules without telling us?"

"You mean about making sound?"

"Of course!"

Feeling attacked and defensive, and not wanting to feel I'd made a mistake while turning the rule-breaking into such an elegant teaching moment, I replied to her by explaining my pedagogy. "Well," I said, "you know it's impossible for a teacher to tell his students to break the rules because that becomes a new rule. Breaking the rules is something students have to find on their own."

"I see. So when you set up the silence rule, you were really just waiting for someone to break it?"

"No," I said, rather weakly. By this time I knew I was on the wrong track, but I didn't know where I'd gone wrong.

"But you knew someone might?"

"Someone might."

"And then, if they do, you praise them, right? And you let those of us who've been taking the rules seriously realize we're just idiots."

"No, I didn't say that."

"Of course not. You didn't *say* that. That's just what you *meant*."

"I don't think you're an idiot. In fact, I think you're doing wonderful work. It was not less so because you did not break the silence."

"Oh," she said, "Thanks."

For a minute, we both sat in silence. Then she spoke about how often she'd gotten in trouble as a child for breaking rules, and how distrustful she'd become of teachers and rules in general. By the time she left, I think we both sighed a sigh of relief: She no longer felt I was one more in a long line of treasonous teachers, and I felt hopeful that I had not poisoned the trust she had in me and in the work.

But that evening, I kept thinking about what had happened, rolling it over and over in my mind and trying to figure out where I'd gone wrong. I knew that for the roaring student—and for many of the others in the final circle—the lesson about rule-breaking had been an important one. I'd been right, I still felt, not to interrupt his roars, and right to use the occasion to talk about rule-breaking. Where I'd gone off-track, I realized, was when I'd failed to respond to the startled look on this young woman's face. I'd known even then that something was bothering her, but I'd felt so good about my "rule-breaking" speech, I hadn't wanted to ruin a good moment.

When this student had challenged what I'd done in class, rather than responding to the plea she was making, rather than just listening to her tone of voice and perceiving what she needed, I'd set about defending myself by explaining my pedagogy, as if I thought of myself as infallible—the perfect teacher whose every lesson is well thought-out, whose every word is spoken on purpose. How hard would it have been for me just to say, "You're right. Maybe I made a mistake there"? But in that moment, it had somehow seemed terribly difficult for me to admit to being wrong.

Culture, mistakes and forgiveness

Composer Arnold Schoenberg once wrote:

> The teacher must have the courage to be wrong. His task is not to prove infallible, knowing everything and never going wrong, but rather inexhaustible, ever seeking and perhaps, sometimes finding. Why want to be a demigod? Why not, rather, be a complete man?
> (from Schoenberg's *Harminielehre*, in Christensen, 1982, p. xiv)

Part of the answer to Schoenberg's question is that, on top of our general, cultural fear of failure, we teachers feel a special responsibility to be "good examples" to our students. The irony here, as Mary Field Belenky points out, is that students also need examples that there are "no mistakes":

> Students need opportunities to watch ... professors solve (and fail to solve) problems. They need models of thinking as a human, imperfect, and attainable activity.
> (Belenky, et al., 1986, p. 217)

Not to mention the fact that even teachers may deserve the "gentle, loving permission to make mistakes—to be a beloved child, loved no matter how much we goof" (Ristad, 1982, p. 143).

In *Saint Nadie in Winter,* Terrance Keenan reminds us that this difficulty we have with making mistakes is, in part, a cultural one, for there are other cultures that deal quite differently with mistakes and with misdeeds.

> A theater troupe in my town, The Open Hand Theater, runs the International Puppet and Mask Museum. In their collection is a wooden helmet mask from West Africa, which has a carved snake surrounding it. The snake is not there as a symbol of evil, as we might construe it in the West. It is there because it sheds its skin and renews itself, leaving the old skin behind. In the community of its origin there is a ceremony for when a member of the community commits a crime or major transgression against it. The individual is compelled to wear the mask and in doing so becomes the snake. He

or she is allowed to shed his or her skin of the old life. All that went on is left behind and forgotten, dead. Life begins anew. Everyone shares in this rebirth, in this leaving behind. They collectively forget the individual's old skin, old life of error, and accept the new person as one of them, giving him or her a new name. One is given a second chance. The past is dead. There is no blame.

(Keenan, 2001, p. 68)

In addition to our cultural prejudices against failure, and in addition to the teacherly responsibility we feel, there are even more reasons why we have such great difficulty forgiving ourselves—and others—for mistakes. One is that, like listening, accepting a mistake is not something one can "do;" it is not a positive action we can force upon our students or ourselves (Don't feel bad about that mistake! No, stop feeling bad right now!). It is a not an "action" at all but a surrender to a natural process of recovery, a process our culture has encumbered with the weight of sin and of guilt.

Another reason mistakes are difficult to tolerate is that we have learned that the most acceptable procedure for *undoing* mistakes is an arduous and onerous one. Our religions encourage us to demonstrate forgiveness, but they also caution us that forgiveness is difficult and painful. Mistakes, after all, are sins, and sins require atonement or recompense.[1] So, while each of the Abrahamic religions describes a different road to forgiveness, none suggests that it might be an easy, natural process. Those who do misdeeds must atone or repent or be punished in the prescribed manner before they are "granted" forgiveness or absolution.

Moreover, in addition to these high cultural hurdles to the letting go of mistakes, I am beginning to suspect that there is still another impediment: a perverse sort of pleasure we obtain from holding on to our feelings of guilt. Here's what I mean:

Forgiving oneself

It was March. A gray, windy day on the Friday of a hard week, after a long cold winter. During my morning class, I'd caught myself staring out the window, staring at my watch, staring at the door. The previous

---

1 Perhaps this is because, in our culture, all of life is seen as an extension of business economics: the mistakes we make are debts; and debts must be repaid. Both "failure" and "surrender" are concepts our American culture teaches us to avoid. For a further examination of the difficulties we have with these non-activities and with forgiveness, see my two articles about the writing of *The Laramie Project* in *Psychoanalytic Dialogues* (Wangh, 2005).

evening, I'd had to chair our apartment co-op meeting, a meeting that had climaxed with two elderly couples complaining to each other about which one of them had been to blame for a leak in the heating pipes, which had dripped through the hallway ceiling—15 years before. So I was not at my best. During the morning class, my comments on the students' work were terse, my smile in our feedback circle forced, my body slightly collapsed. At the end of class one of the young women in the class came up to me as I was slipping out the door to ask if I was all right.

"Just tired," I said, thinking: Shit, they knew.

During the midday break, I quickly threw away the tuna sandwiches I'd made for my lunch and treated myself to tempura udon in the hopes its warmth might get me through the afternoon class. The first scene in the afternoon group was good, very good. Not only did the scene itself go well, but more importantly, the students who presented it were able to give themselves accurate and helpful feedback. I didn't really have much to add to what the actors said about the scene, so I spoke about the value of learning to give oneself positive feedback. Inwardly, I allowed myself to think perhaps I was earning my pay.

The second scene of the afternoon was a disaster. It seemed not to have progressed at all since the previous week.

"Did you two rehearse this?" I asked, marginally aware of the critical tone in my voice.

"Yes, twice," said the young man.

"Once," corrected his scene partner. "Remember. The room was being used."

"But we did it in the hall."

"And what happened to the blocking you'd created last week?" I asked.

"But what were we supposed to do? Someone had taken the room. We'd signed up, but there was some show rehearsing in there. Some faculty directed show. What could we do?"

"You could have scheduled another rehearsal."

"We tried," said the girl. "We made a time on Sunday."

"I couldn't be there."

"You might at least have called."

"I did call."

"Four hours later."

"Yeah. Sorry."

On any other day, I might have been able to transform this dialogue into a teachable moment, something helpful. But on this day, no wisdom shone through my overcast mood.

"Ricki," I said, not quite knowing where I was going, "last week I spent fifteen minutes getting you into your body, helping you put the gestures in your hands, but today you were holding your arms at your sides again."

"I was?"

"Yes. And holding on to the chair again."

"Oh, yeah. I guess."

"You guess?"

"Yeah."

Then I lost it.

"This work is not about guessing. It is about learning to see what you are doing while you are doing it. It is about being present, not absent. It's your responsibility."

"But what were we supposed to do, the room was ... "

"So maybe you have to get up early on Sunday morning, like Sondra said."

"I couldn't make it."

"I'm just the teacher, you know. All I can do is point to the path. You've got to walk down the road."

"I'm sorry," said Ricki. Suddenly he was on the edge of tears. "I ... I couldn't come in on Sunday morning."

"And you couldn't call?"

"They were arresting my father."

Ricki's words filled the air in the room with a great, silence. Everybody was wondering the same thing, but no one breathed.

"I'm sorry," said his scene partner. "I didn't ... you didn't ... "

"Yeah," said Ricki.

My mind was scrambling, spinning, trying to get a grip, the way your feet do when a bicycle slips out of gear. "I'm sorry, Ricki," I began. But I knew I had to do better than that. "I ... I should have asked you what was going on for you."

"No, that's okay."

"No, there was no need for me to yell at you in any case." There was a pause. No one spoke. "There are things more important than scene-work." Again silence. "Let's just sit here for a minute together," I added, hoping it was the right thing to do, but no longer trusting myself at all. Thankfully the class time was almost over. We all sat in silence for a minute—in retrospect that was the one thing I got right.

In that silent circle I thought: everything I'd said had been true; it *had* been a waste of our time for him to present the scene without having worked on it. But the fact that what I said was true did not make it appropriate, and it was patently obvious that my words had not been helpful. Worse still, I'd displayed my temper in front of the whole class. But the damage was done. Now I had myself to contend with.

After dismissing the class, I walked into the teacher lounge, grateful to find it empty. How could I have been so stupid? What had I been thinking? Was I thinking at all? And if not, why wasn't I thinking? God, I thought, I've been teaching for nearly thirty years. How could I have done what I'd done, said what I said? Maybe I needed to go back into therapy? Maybe I should find another profession?

I left the building, but I didn't want to go home, so I walked onto the streets of New York, wandering east, crossing crowded streets, noticing no one, seeing only the walls, the garbage, the old, soot-covered snow.

I needed to stare at a little piece of emptiness, and the only way to do that in Manhattan is to get yourself to a river. On the way, the empty lots, the graffitied walls and the overflowing garbage cans of the East Village corroborated my bleak mood. Finally I crossed over the FDR on the 6th Street overpass and into what passes in New York City for a park: a few battered baseball diamonds, their fences festooned with scraps of plastic, a mud-caked soccer field, and hundreds of yards of cracked concrete pathways punctuated by ice-covered puddles. As I walked toward the iron fence at the water's edge I passed two giant pieces of cardboard, shards of what must once have been the box for a new refrigerator. How odd, I thought. Why would anyone have a refrigerator delivered to the East River? This cardboard, I thought, is the coup de grace: ugliness without excuse, ugliness for its own sake.

I turned toward the water. The tide was racing out. The East River was roiling south making blue-black waves; some even had whitecaps. I stared across the water at the bare docks of the Brooklyn Navy Yard, distant and cold. The whole scene matched my mood perfectly. I saw myself as a figure in a painting by some artist whose pallet was restricted to shades of gray. The man in this picture, I thought, is a teacher who prided himself on listening, but has managed to heartlessly insult a student whose father was just arrested. As a teacher, I gave myself an F. I gave the artist an F too, for wasting his paint on me.

Then suddenly, behind my back, I heard high-pitched yelling, screaming, and laughter. I turned to see a group of four or five kids, boys eight to twelve years old, who were using the giant pieces of cardboard to pull each other along the frozen puddles. Sleds, I realized, they're sleds. That's what the cardboard box is doing here.

The kids had a system: two would sit on the cardboard platter, and two others would run along either side of a long, narrow ice-puddle, pulling the edges of the box, picking up speed and then, just before the end of the puddle, giving the sled riders a push and a spin. All of them were laughing now, demanding faster runs: "Ma' rapido! Ma' rapido!"

I stood leaning against the river railing, watching these kids for fifteen minutes as the daylight faded and the park pathway lights came on. Once, one of the older boys spun the cardboard too fast and a small boy flew off, fell on his forehead and started to cry. But when the older boy—his brother, perhaps—offered him an extra ride on his lap, his cries subsided immediately and, within a minute, both of them were laughing again.

It took me much longer to let go of my pain and get back on my sled: even though our class spent time in processing what we'd all been through; even though Ricki's scene was much improved; and even though, when I talked with Ricki privately, he didn't seem resentful. Clearly I was off the hook, and yet for weeks I held on, unable to forgive myself for what I'd done that day.

I tried to think it through: It had been a rotten week. Ricki hadn't done his work, and how in hell could I have known his father had been arrested! And yet, I kept thinking—if only I had been more in control of myself, I might have taught a much better class, and not made such a fool of myself.

That, I realize now, was the issue: control. I hadn't controlled myself properly at the time, but now, as long as I felt guilty, then in fantasy at least, I could control the past. The thought "If only I had acted differently" was painful, but it also permitted me to perpetuate an alternative history in my mind. It gave me the magical power to alter the past. To give up the guilt would mean giving up that control.

How often in this book I have returned to this issue of control, and to the many ways in which our fears of losing control can undermine our own best interests! In the chapter on Questions, I talked about the ill consequences of needing to maintain control of the curriculum. In the chapter on Listening, I recounted how my Balthazar missed his cue because I was trying to hold too tightly to the text. In the chapter on Feedback, I wrote about how Samuel's fears of losing control stifled his acting. Throughout other chapters I've talked about how teachers run into problems when they try to deny or control the feelings they have towards their students. Now it seems this issue has returned once more, cloaked this time in shades of self-deprecation: Powerful? Who, me? Not at all! I'm just feeling guilty for my terrible mistake.

How central this issue of Power and Control seems to many of the problems of pedagogy. Perhaps it's time we looked at it head-on.

Chapter 12

Power and control

The pleasure in complete domination over another person (or other animate creature) is the very essence of the sadistic drive.

Erich Fromm

A leader is best when we hardly know he exists. When his work is done, his aim fulfilled, his followers will say, "We did this ourselves!"

Lao Tzu

When the University of Paris was established in the twelfth century, the teachers at the school were hired by the Church. At the University of Oxford, it was the State and the English Crown who were the employers. But in Bologna, where the very first degree-granting university in the world had been established in 1088, it was the students who were in charge; it was the students who hired the faculty and determined what should be taught.

On some level, this is still, actually, the underlying situation: Through tuition or taxes, it is the students (or their parents) who are the employers while the teachers are mere employees. However, nowadays teachers can be mightily offended when it appears that students might actually exercise some of their latent power. In a recent *New York Times* Op Ed piece, Stanley Fish decried the tyranny of the students in Texas whose teacher evaluations will be used by college administrators to help determine faculty tenure.

> The idea is to hold "tenured professors more accountable" … and what they will be accountable to are not professional standards but the preferences of their students, who, in advance of being instructed, are presumed to be authorities on how best they should be taught.[1]

---

1 http://opinionator.blogs.nytimes.com. If you look up Fish's Op Ed, I recommend reading the reader comments too that follow the piece. Fish responds to some of these comments

Fish is not alone in his umbrage. Several years ago, when I was a member of the Academic Affairs Committee at the Tisch School of the Arts at NYU, the committee heard complaints from several part-time faculty members who said they lived with the fear that if they gave students low grades, the students would write negative evaluations, and that as a consequence they, as untenured faculty, would not be rehired for the next year.

If such teacher evaluation systems leave teachers fearful of their students' power, they mistake the situation; for these devices do not really empower the students. They are procedures designed by the administration to monitor and manage the faculty, for in most schools nowadays, it is the administration, not the students or the teachers, who hold the real power. The apparent power struggle between the students and the faculty simply veils this underlying reality. In 1964, I had the great good fortune of being present when, for a moment, this veil was drawn aside.

In the fall of that year I was a graduate English student at the University of California when Mario Savio, another Berkeley student, climbed on top of a police car that had entered the campus to arrest another student activist. From the top of the car, Savio described the realities of the situation to the hundreds of students who had initiated a sit-down strike outside the administration building. The students had petitioned the school President, Clark Kerr, to change the school's policy, which forbid the setting up of tables to hand out political literature on school property. Kerr had responded to them by saying that he could not go against the policy of the Board of Regents: "Would you ever imagine the manager of a firm making a statement publicly in opposition to his board of directors?" he asked. To this, Savio responded:

> If this is a firm, and if the Board of Regents are the board of directors, and if President Kerr in fact is the manager, then I'll tell you something: the faculty are a bunch of employees, and we're the raw material! But we're a bunch of raw material that don't mean to have any process upon us, don't mean to be made into any product, don't mean to end up being bought by some clients of the University, be they the government, be they industry, be they organized labor, be they anyone! We're human beings![2]

in his follow up: http://opinionator.blogs.nytimes.com/2010/06/28/student-evaluations-part-two/?scp=3&sq=stanley%20fish,%20texas,%20evaluations&st=cse

2 http://www.fsm-a.org/stacks. This quotation is from the speech Mario Savio made before the Free Speech Movement demonstrators at Sproul Plaza on the campus of the University of California at Berkeley on December 3, 1964.

The Free Speech Movement was the start of an anomalous few years of clarity about who held power in the University. During the next few years, students at many colleges across the country actually exercised their power, holding strikes and organizing "teach-ins," inviting speakers who could speak about "real-world" issues such as racial segregation and the war in Viet Nam, and putting pressure on school administrations to create Women's Studies and African American Studies departments, hire minority faculty, and eliminate ROTC programs on many campuses. Student strikes were instrumental in forcing Lyndon Johnson out of office and may even have hastened the end of the war in Viet Nam. (Wasn't that a time!)

Nowadays, however, neither students nor faculty feel much power. In the classroom where it matters, most students feel it is the teachers who hold sway. After all, it is the teachers who make the rules, the teachers who tell students what they must study, and the teachers who hand out the grades.

Meanwhile, teachers find themselves faced with twin paradoxes. First, they often feel they have no power over what they must teach. They are required by the administration, and/or the state to cover a curriculum they have not chosen. Yet, to do their jobs at all, they must control their classes and *act* powerful. Then there is the deeper paradox inherent in the act of teaching itself: The fact that the ultimate purpose of all education is to help students come into their own power, and yet, the only route to that goal is to exercise power over the students. It is this second paradox I propose to look at now: Is there a way for us to wield our power that simultaneously empowers the students over whom we wield it?

Bare knuckles

In the previous chapters I've suggested that in working with fear, resistance, transference, or erotic energy, the first step is for the teacher to become aware of what's going on. I think the same is true with power. We've got to be up-front, with our students and with ourselves, about the power we have.

Two years ago, when I was traveling in Indonesia, a man there told me about a teacher in Java who had forced some of his grade school students to stand on one leg in the sun for hours. He was reprimanded only after one of his students fainted. In America, we no longer hear stories about that kind of abuse in school, but there are teachers who wield their power with malicious glee, even in the arts.

For many years Stella Adler, who had been a leading lady in the Group Theater and had studied with Constantine Stanislavski himself, ran an acting studio in New York City. Acting teacher Pam Rickard, who once studied with Adler, relates this story about Stella's teaching style:

> A young man got up to work solo. It was early in the fall so we were working on entrances with objectives and obstacles. He was onstage for maybe 30 seconds. He was clearly having a hard time fulfilling the exercise. Suddenly Stella clapped her hands in fury. "Get off the stage" she yelled. "Get off the stage and don't get back on until you know what you are doing." The young man left. He never came back. The studio was silent. No one dared to move a muscle.
>
> Stella then turned to us and smiled. Her tone changed to become almost sweet and grandmotherly. Her moods were capricious. "You see my darlings. If you can endure Conservatory, you have what it takes to be an actor."
>
> (Rickard, 2010)

When Pam Rickard told me this story, I was reminded of an acting class I'd attended while I was a graduate directing student, a class taught by a teacher who often drank liquor from a flask while teaching. One day, deep in his cups, and disappointed with the work a young actress had presented in her scene, he insulted the student until she was in tears. Then he told her to perform again—to demonstrate how effective her tears could be in the work.

Some teachers are proud of their dictatorial teaching style. When Eva Mekler, the author of *The New Generation of Acting Teachers*, asked acting teacher Elinor Renfield, "How do you help students cope with stage fright?" Renfield replied:

> I yell. I say, "What the hell are you doing in this class if you have stage fright?" What the hell can I do? Sometimes I get very tyrannical with certain students. They need it and ask for it.
>
> (Mekler, 1988, pp. 152–53)

I've heard similar stories about ballet masters, orchestra conductors, and stage directors who like to play the tyrant. Frankly, I don't get it. Although some professional performers can shrug off such treatment, for many others—and certainly for young students—both the performer's joy in the process and the performance itself will suffer from such abuse. On the other hand, in one way, such a blatantly dictatorial style has one advantage for the students: it leaves no doubt about where the power sits. In a class run by an autocrat, you know what you're in for. Many teachers, however, are less up-front—or simply less aware—about how they exercise their power.

Kid gloves

A few years ago I overheard a conversation in a school hallway between a teacher—a woman who prided herself on always being a good friend to her students—and a young actress who had apparently felt misunderstood in class.

"Why did you have to say that?" the student was saying, through her tears.

"What did I say, honey?"

"You said it was time to move on. Couldn't you see I hadn't finished?"

"Do you think I don't see what's going on in my class?"

"No ... I just ... "

"You feel that I'm insensitive?"

"No ... of course not."

"So, did I do something I should feel bad about?"

What could the student say? She'd been looking for some understanding and sympathy from the teacher, but the teacher had turned the tables on her now and was asking *her* for sympathy. "No," the student replied.

"Good," the teacher said. "You're doing very good work, you know." And then she walked away, leaving the student with a stunned look on her face.

In this situation, the teacher certainly didn't feel powerful. Quite the opposite: after all, she was being criticized, and so to defend herself she turned the tables on the student, making it seem as though it was the student who had the power to pass judgment on *her*. Then the teacher had sealed the moment with a compliment, a move that reasserted the teacher's power while making it virtually impossible for the student to remonstrate. How could she be angry at someone who was praising her? The teacher had maintained her own power by seeming to give it up! In this way, unacknowledged power can be even more manipulative than the naked kind.

Being unaware of one's power is not the same as not wielding it—certainly not from the students' point of view. Even if the power we wield is not power we desire, even if it is a power that the educational institution has imposed upon us—like the power to give grades—it is, nevertheless, something our students experience, and therefore it is a power we must not obscure. Peter Elbow writes:

> I feel that I can best minimize this power relationship by getting the weapons on the table. Trying to pretend that the power and

weapons are not there—however swinging I am and however
groovy the students are—only gets the power more permanently
into the air.

(Elbow, 1986, p. 79)

When Linda Putnam and I founded the Acting Growth Program in
Boston, Massachusetts, we tried to be groovy. This was 1973 you
understand, so being groovy was quite normal, and at that time it did
not seem particularly outlandish when we declared that at our new
acting school everyone, teachers and students alike, would have an
equal voice. To facilitate this egalitarian process, we instituted long,
full-group meetings every other week at which everyone could be heard
on all sorts of issues. The system worked well—for questions such as
what time should classes should start, or how long our lunch break
should be—but within a few months it became clear that this procedure
was not practical for other decisions, such as how many hours the
teachers should teach, or what the curriculum should be. Bit by
bit it became clear that the idea that we could all share equally in
decisions that affected us so differently was a myth, a pleasing fiction
that masked the unpleasant reality that the teacher–student playing
field is not an even pitch. Peter Elbow calls what we tried to do a
"bamboozle":

> There are two things which teachers often do that help bamboozle
> students into this distrust of rationality: teachers hide authority and
> run away from their authority, and in both cases allow rationality
> to serve as a smoke screen to mask the process, fooling both themselves
> and their students.
>
> (Elbow, 1986 p. 91)

I don't think Linda and I tried to hide our authority, but we probably
did try to run away from it. In 1973 wielding power made me very
uncomfortable—perhaps because it would have meant admitting to
myself how much I actually *did* like being in control. So, seeming to share
power, while it may have appeared generous, was actually a self-protective
ploy—a power move.

Mary Rose O'Reilley writes:

> When I was a young teacher, I used to think the student-centered
> classroom was predicated on diffusion of power. As a pacifist, I
> was eager to give it away. I found this to be dangerous and con-
> fusing to students. Whether we like it or not as teachers, we have

inherited our fathers' lightsaber, and we have to learn how to use it. The worst thing we can do is pretend we don't have the power.

(O'Reilley, 1993, pp. 71–72)

By abdicating power we leave a vacuum, and what is more, we set a bad example for our students, many of whom are in search of positive examples of how lightsabers should be wielded. Often enough, even those students who seem outwardly assertive may be having a hard time acknowledging their own power to themselves.

The fear of being powerful

Cecelia had been a "difficult" student ever since she'd arrived at the program. She was an accomplished comedienne, but she often used her comic abilities to protect herself from deep emotional experiences. Again and again, I'd encourage her to take more time, or to allow whatever she was feeling under the surface to inhabit her whole body, or even just to stop and name what she was feeling. But she always had a joke at the ready, or some other way to duck out of the discomfort that feeling a strong emotion seemed to evoke in her.

Now we were working on Shakespeare monologues, and it was happening again; only now, since this was Shakespeare, the disconnect between the power of the words she was speaking and Cecelia's behavior was undeniable. She was playing Portia, Brutus' wife in *Julius Caesar*. Portia's speech to Brutus is one of mounting anguish, and Cecelia's rendition was strong—up to a point.

> ... and what men tonight
> Have had resort to you; for here have been
> Some six or seven, who did hide their faces
> Even from the darkness.

But as Portia became more and more desperate, strangely enough Cecelia began to smile, and her hands began to shake as she said:

> Tell me Brutus,
> Is it excepted that I should know no secrets
> That appertain to you? Am I your self
> But as it were in sort or limitation,
> To keep with you at meals, comfort your bed,
> And talk to you sometimes?

By the time she came to the end of Portia's speech, Cecelia sounded frustrated but she was almost laughing. At the end of her showing, after she'd spoken to the group about how dissatisfied she'd been with her performance and about the waves of disgust and fear she'd experienced doing it, I suggested we try going through the piece again, but very slowly this time. Just as she got up to start, I asked her, "Is there something you're afraid of here, now, even as we begin to work?"

She thought for a moment. "I guess I'm afraid of being bad," she said. "I'm afraid my acting will just suck, big time." And she laughed again.

"Okay," I said, "Let's just begin at the top."

Again, as Cecelia reached the middle of the speech, the same thing happened.

"Can I look at the text?" I asked. "Oh, I see."

"You mean I cut Brutus' line there? Well, I thought, you know, turning it into a monologue ... "

"No, I don't mean the cut. I mean what Brutus says: 'Kneel not, gentle Portia.' Have you tried actually kneeling at that point?"

"No. I mean that would feel kind of over-the-top, you know."

We began again, but this time, when her hands began to shake again, I said, "Stand it. You can stand it." As she reached the climax of the speech, I added, "Now, just let your knees buckle." As she began to kneel, I gently placed my hand on her back.

> ... Tell me Brutus,
> Is it excepted that I should know no secrets
> That appertain to you? Am I your self
> But as it were in sort or limitation,
> To keep with you at meals, comfort your bed,
> And talk to you sometimes?

By this point, tears were streaming down Cecelia's face, again her hands began to shake, so I added, "Try reaching out."

Her voice cracked as the power of the character and the desperation of Portia's situation overtook her. Instead of holding back from being "over-the-top," Cecelia was allowing herself to be inhabited by Portia's weakness, and in doing so, she found her own strength. At the end, the students in the audience broke into applause.

The next day, Cecelia took me aside and said, "I want to tell you something. You remember when you asked me yesterday was there something I was afraid of. Well, I lied. Actually what I was most afraid of—but was too embarrassed to say out loud—was being good, really good."

Her comment reminded me that, along the *via negativa*, one of the most common fears performers encounter is the fear of being too large, too powerful, or too "good" on stage. It is a difficult demon to uproot, because it often accosts an actor in the guise of kindly, mannerly advice—"Let's not show off." "Don't push." Or "Careful, now. No overacting!"—advice whose tone seems to carry the most generous intentions, but whose effect is to deprive both the performer and her audience of the satisfaction that comes only with full commitment to each gesture, each phrase, each emotion on stage.

As Marianne Williamson wrote:

> Our deepest fear is not that we are inadequate. Our deepest fear is that we are powerful beyond measure. It is our light, not our darkness, that most frightens us. We ask ourselves, who am I to be brilliant, gorgeous, talented, and fabulous? Actually, who are you not to be? You are a child of God. Your playing small doesn't serve the world. There's nothing enlightened about shrinking so that other people won't feel insecure around you. We are all meant to shine, as children do. We are born to make manifest the glory of God that is within us. It's not just in some of us, it's in everyone. And as we let our own light shine, we unconsciously give other people permission to do the same. As we are liberated from our own fear, our presence automatically liberates others.
>
> (Williamson, 1992, p. 191)

Easier said than done. For most of us have been encouraged for years *not* to "shine, as children do." As a consequence, I've often seen acting students shy away from bowing to the audience and receiving applause they deserve at the end of a performance. It just feels too good to bear.

Music teacher Eloise Ristad would sometimes challenge students who were contending with this fear to ask themselves the question: "What does my problem buy for me?"

> Does my problem with performing insure a comfortable anonymity instead of a challenging career as a concert violinist? ... Am I honestly immobilized by my problems, or terrified by the possibility of success?
>
> (Ristad, 1982, pp. 153–54)

Confronted with the "possibility of success," a performer faces a moment rather like the one every child encounters when he first learns to stand and walk alone. While on the one hand he acquires an exciting independence, on the other hand (or *from* the other hand) he loses his mother.

For a performer to allow herself to really shine, she must let go of her self-denigration, and of her long-accustomed dependency upon the teacher.

Meanwhile, the teacher must tolerate a corresponding loss; for when your student comes into her own power, she doesn't need you anymore. As James Wilkinson puts it: "The final aim of ... education is to make the student independent of the teacher" (Wilkinson, 1982, p. 8). Or as Zen Master Lin Chi said, "If you meet the Buddha, kill the Buddha. If you meet a Patriarch, kill the Patriarch." In this formulation, our role as teachers is to play the patriarchs ... waiting to be killed.

NEOTENY

The human propensity for dependency is the direct result of what biologists call "neoteny," the unfinished nature of the human body and mind at birth and prolonged nature of our infancy. More than any other animal, human babies are born helpless, and they remain physically dependent upon their parents for years.

> As the [evolutionary] battle was to be won by brain rather than brawn, some kind of dramatic evolutionary step had to be taken to greatly increase [human] brain-power. What happened was rather odd: the hunting ape became an infantile ape. This evolutionary trick is not unique; it has happened in a number of quite separate cases. Put very simply, it is a process (called neoteny) by which certain juvenile or infantile characters are retained and prolonged into adult life.
>
> (Morris, 1967, pp. 32–33)

Human neoteny is necessary because the head is so large at nine months gestation that if it the fetus spent any more time in the womb, it wouldn't be able to get out at all. In order for human beings to evolve larger brains—without human females having to evolve wider pelvises, which might have interfered with early humans' need to travel long distances (see below)—human pregnancy had to be shortened. So, unlike other mammals who are born capable of walking within minutes of birth, and other primates who can at least hold on to their mothers from the first, human infants are born unfinished, before their bodies have acquired any of the muscular capabilities they will need to maintain life outside the womb—except for sucking.

> A young chimpanzee completes its brain-growth within twelve months after birth. Our own species, by contrast, has at birth a brain which is only twenty-three per cent of its final adult size. Rapid growth continues for a further six years after birth, and the whole growing process is not complete until about the twenty-third year of life.
>
> (Morris, 1967, pp. 32–33)

For this infantile neoteny to work, human adults (mostly mothers) had to be capable of traveling long distances on two legs, leaving an arm free to carry the infant and lift it to the breast when it cried. Adult humans had to be willing to feed and care for the child for many, many years before it would be capable of getting food and fending for itself.

For homosapiens to survive, this burden was a necessity. Individuals born without this instinct would leave no progeny. For human children, this situation has been a mixed blessing. On the one hand, it is our slow growing brain, and its ability to keep learning, that makes humans a "higher" form of life than other animals. On the other hand, the fact that we humans must spend so many years so very dependent upon our elders means that we have a long, long time to learn that we are incapable of self-sufficiency, that we are dependent for our sustenance, for warmth, and for knowledge upon others. No matter what particular culture, religion, world-view, or language a child is taught, the universal lesson each one learns is: You are dependent upon others for everything that matters.

Schooling extends this double-edged lesson. On the one hand it teaches us "survival skills"—in America that means the importance of self-reliance—but as it does so, it also reiterates and reifies the lesson of our dependency, encouraging us to look (up) to teachers as providers of knowledge, and to feel ignorant and incompetent in comparison to our mentors.

Freedom is acquired by conquest

Now let us look at one more paradox, the great paradox this whole chapter has hinted at: that even when you know that your students are ready to take the final step towards their liberation, it won't work to tell them so, for power cannot be given, it must be taken. Or, as Paulo Freire puts it: "Freedom is acquired by conquest, not by gift" (Freire,

1999, p. 29). If you open the door for your student to leave, you deprive him of that exquisite mixture of sorrow and satisfaction that arises only from opening the door for one's self.

It is really very tricky, this power business. We hide our power even as we exercise it. We hold on to it even when we try to give it away. And if we're doing our jobs properly, behind every lesson we teach, lies the meta-lesson: You don't need a teacher.

One year, during my graduate directing studies at NYU, I took an acting class with Lloyd Richards. This was the first scene-study class I'd taken that left me feeling really good about my own acting work, and I remember approaching Lloyd on the last day of class and asking, "Do you think I have what it takes to be an actor?"

His answer was, "I can't tell you that."

In my insecurity, I took that to be a euphemistic, "No." But perhaps Lloyd was simply saying exactly what he meant: that my question was one *he* could not answer. It was a question I must ask myself. But, like many students, I read meaning into what Lloyd did *not* say. So, another lesson I draw from this memory is that silence speaks loudly—but what silence does say is often open to interpretation.

Chapter 13

Silence

Radical teachers possess the capacity to listen well and the self-control not to always fill silence with the sound of their own voices.

Pamela Annas

silence ... respects understanding ... silence gives that sense to all there is ... Silence is so windowful.

Gertrude Stein

Our fourth grade art teacher, Mrs. Lord, was always telling us to fill in the sky. I wanted to move on to another painting, but Lordy would say, "Why don't you finish the painting you've made, Stevie? The sky isn't just white, now is it? Why don't you fill in the sky?"

I wish I'd known about John Cage or Beckett back then. Maybe I could have explained to Mrs. Lord that the emptiness of my sky helped to focus the eye on the exploding Russian MIG-23 I'd drawn. But this was 1953, and in fourth grade all I could think was that filling in the sky would mean wasting a whole lot of blue paint. It would be boring, even more boring than painting class was already. So, in a way, I agreed with Lordy: empty space was boring, and boredom was a bad thing—it gave you time to realize how boring school was, and what was the point anyway?

A central undertaking, perhaps *the* central undertaking of the twentieth century, was the elimination of boredom. Boredom came to be seen as a serious disorder, a cancer upon the healthy, productive use of time, an illness to be cured at all costs. Although the costs have been terrific, we mostly don't notice them because we're too busy; we don't have the time.

The attack upon empty time began as a simple economic imperative: the faster anything could be moved or manufactured or cooked or written, the more money could be made. But this idea—the idea that time not filled with activity is time wasted—spread from the work-place to all other arenas of life. Each moment nowadays must be filled with useful activity, or at least with *some* activity.

By the end of the nineteenth century, the mad rush of modern culture was on. Even as most people acquiesced to the cultural pressure to move faster and faster, some artists began to push back, and began searching for ways to help their audiences become aware of the importance of emptiness. In 1897 the French poet, Stéphane Mallarmé, utterly transformed poetry by spreading the words of his great poem "A Throw of the Dice" across the space of the page. During the following decades, even as the workaday world kept speeding up, several artists began to insist upon the importance of empty space and time. In the early 1900s the Russian artist Kasimir Malevich created works like "Black Square" and "White on White," which forced the spectator to contemplate what he is *not* seeing. Composers like Berg and Webern began to use silence itself as a compositional element. In 1952 John Cage took the exploration of silence all the way. He composed *4'33"*, during which the audience listens to silence—and whatever fills their personal experience of silence— for four minutes and thirty-three seconds. Cage said later "The sound experience which I prefer to all others is the experience of silence" (Sebestik, 1992).

In the theater, it was Thornton Wilder's *Our Town*, written in 1938, that first made full use of silence. *Our Town* is a play almost without dramatic tension, an exciting, heart-rending, beautiful play about— nothing. Or rather, about how very much is happening when nothing is happening, a play about the exquisite expressiveness of silence. The most dramatic scene of the play—if one can call it "dramatic"—is the love scene at the soda fountain, in which the two young lovers, George and Emily, stumble over their words and finally express their love by not mentioning it:

GEORGE: Emily, if I *do* improve and make a big change ... would you be ... I mean: *could* you be ...
EMILY: I ... I am now; I always have been.
GEORGE: (*pause*) So, I guess this is an important talk we've been having.
EMILY: Yes ... yes.

(Wilder, 1938, 1957, p. 74)

At the end of *Our Town*, Emily revisits her childhood and observes, "It goes so fast. We don't have time to look at one another" (Wilder, 1938, 1957, p. 110).

The reason life goes by so fast is that the human mind—like that of other animals who must survive by noticing movement—is designed to look for the action, and it takes some learning (or some *un*learning) to perceive the negative space or the silence. To do so the mind must learn to let go of the exciting, active elements:

- The eye must let go of the line and the movement.
- The ear must let go of the note.
- The heart must let go of the desire.

That's not easy for most of us to do. In the final moments of *Our Town*, Emily asks: "Do any human beings ever realize life while they live it?—every, every minute?"

The Stage Manager answers: "No. (*Pause.*) The saints and poets, maybe—they do some" (Wilder, 1938, 1957, p. 110).

Silent learning

In several chapters in this book I've suggested that, in one way or another, teachers in the arts must set an example of each artistic quality they expect their students to emulate. But silence is not a capacity in which most teachers have been schooled.

I grew up in the 1950s, and until I was 14, our house had no television. I listened to the radio. My favorite shows were *The Answer Man* and *The Lone Ranger*. We always had dinner at exactly 6:20 when my father finished with his last psychoanalytic patient, came out of the office at the front of the apartment, and expected dinner to be ready on the table. But on Wednesdays, *The Lone Ranger* came on at 7:00. If dinner wasn't finished, I'd beg to turn on the radio anyway, since the alternative was to sit in the deadly silence of our dinner table where nothing was said but: "How was school today?" "Fine." And, "Can I have some more potatoes." The radio provided a respite from the oppressiveness of that silence. On the radio there was never a silence because on the radio, silence is a sin: Dead Air.

It was the same in school, except that in school I felt it was *my* responsibility to guard against the sin of dead air. When the teacher asked a question, I *had* to raise my hand. It was automatic. If there were several hands waving, it was a competition. If there were no other hands, I felt I must put mine up. Not to do so would have been unthinkable, it would have been like letting down the whole class, and the teacher. Moreover, speaking up in class provided a moment of recognition—a short-acting appreciation-fix, the effect of which wore off as soon as the teacher asked the next question.

A thick space

With my own habits of speaking up so well ingrained, it never occurred to me when I started teaching, that the silent students in my class might actually have a lot to say, or that I might learn something by paying more attention to their silence. A few years ago, a student of mine completely altered my perception.

Deirdre had come to study at the MFA in Contemporary Performance program at Naropa University already a poet, a teacher, and a very articulate person, so I was surprised to notice that in my pedagogy class, when we entered group discussions, Deirdre often said nothing at all. So after class one day I asked her why she never spoke up in the group. She said it was something she'd been struggling with. The next week she sent me this email:

> I'm noticing that I'm dropping out. I've made this decision that I'm not gonna talk. Or at least some part of me has made this decision. And now that the decision is made, I couldn't talk even if I wanted to. I could say something but probably someone else will say it so I'll let them. I just don't feel like it. It's too much work. I want to run away, shut down, check my email, anything so I don't have to feel this shame. I could say something now. B. just said what I was going to say. Shit. Now I have nothing to say. T. is so bright and alive. ... How does she do that? I felt so energized by the end of class because of what I didn't say. I've checked out of thinking actively too. Let someone else do it. ... I have made the decision not to talk. All I think about is how I'm not talking and I should be talking.

I was stunned. What Deirdre was saying was a complete surprise to me. Behind her silence she was experiencing a great waterfall of thoughts and feelings, thoughts I never could have guessed. I immediately started wondering if there was some way I could address Deirdre's conundrum the next time our class met.

At first I thought, maybe we could break up into small groups for our discussion.[1] I often use small groups to help people process an exercise. The problem was that with small groups the full group never hears each comment made, and in my pedagogy class, where everyone gives feedback to one student who has led the teaching session, it is important that everyone hear everything that is said. So small group discussions wouldn't work.

1 Studies show that in groups of three or four, people participate almost equally, but that in groups larger than four "there is a long tail of participants whose participation is very small" (Light & Cox, 2001, p. 124).

Thomas Kasulis, a teacher who has studied this problem, suggests that one way to encourage participation by silent students is for a teacher to change his manner of calling on people to speak:

> One does not have to call on the first person who volunteers, nor the second, nor the third. In fact, one may have to wait a few moments until the more deliberate thinkers have the chance to formulate their answers. ... the teacher should not be embarrassed to wait if there are no immediate volunteers to answer a question. Often it takes time to think through a response.
>
> (Kasulis, 1982, pp. 41–42)

At the time of my work with Deirdre, I hadn't read Kasulis, and I didn't think of this. (In retrospect I realize how ingrained was my assumption that I *must* call on the one who seems most anxious to speak—the one who acts as I once did.) But I did want to try something that might make it easier for Deirdre and the other students who rarely spoke up to participate in the day's discussion. So I tried another form I knew: The students sat in a "fishbowl" arrangement with a small number of students sitting in a small circle within the larger group, making the talking space of the inner group more intimate. If someone on the outside wished to join, she just tapped the shoulder of one of those in the "fishbowl" and took her place. A noble experiment perhaps, but this is the email Deirdre sent me that evening:

> Fishbowl today.
>
> In-the-middle-talk. I made this decision that I wasn't going to talk in class. That's the decision. It's rigid. There's no flexibility around that. There's a part of me saying you gotta go in this is for you come on go in you gotta go in you gotta talk come on come on do it do it just go in just be brave just go in. and the other part saying nono don't go you don't have to go you don't have to do it don't go you don't have to do anything you already decided not to talk.
>
> and on and on
>
> sorry I didn't go in. I could have gone in. I would have had something to say.
>
> I would have to be picked to go in. You'd have to force me to go in. Say ok now it's your turn. ... It's hard enough to lift my hand to speak but to actually get up off my cushion and step into the center that's miles away. It's also harder because I want to be in the center it's juicy in there I want to be in the center circle so it hurts more to not be in. But I just can't get my body to go there. Oh but I can. I choose not to. I choose not to for a reason. ... Must be a good

reason because my body just won't go. I'll only go if someone from the outside gives me a turn. Otherwise it's thick thick thick space I have to get myself through and sometimes usually it's just too thick.

When I received this email from Deirdre, it was my turn to go through a waterfall of thoughts and feelings. Of course I felt badly that I had not been more perceptive and had not found a way to be more helpful. But I also felt moved by Deirdre's insight into her own process, and awed by the intricacies of the human mind. I was astounded by how very differently Deirdre experienced the question "to-speak-or-not-to-speak?" from the way I had experienced the same question when I was a student. For me, not-to-speak would have been, quite literally, a shame. For her, on the other hand, to-speak was an enormous effort: "You'd have to force me to go in." Here was a student whose silence was filled with thoughts, with judgments and counter-judgments, and who was actually aware that one reason she was not speaking was because "it's juicy in there I want to be in the center circle so it hurts more to not be in." How strange, how wondrous, and what a complex business this matter of silence and speaking in class was turning out to be.

Standing silence

Reading over these emails from Deirdre now, I'm acutely aware that even as a teacher I still have a hard time with silence—though I'm sure I'm not the only teacher who does. After all, many of us who now teach were once the very students who felt a need to fill the silence whenever we could. As Anne Dalke remembers:

> When I was a student, I was silent when I had nothing to say. I felt stupid when I was silent. Probably because of such experiences, I tend to read the silence of others in the classroom not just as a lack of interest but as a lack of ability.
>
> (Dalke, 2002, p. 103)

When my acting students struggle with stage fright, I often point out to them that, if some part of their being didn't enjoy being watched, they wouldn't be in theater at all. Similarly, I think it is probably rare for people who don't like the sound of their own voices to become teachers. For me, becoming a teacher has just compounded my childhood pench-ant for filling the dead air by adding two additional incentives: The first is that as a teacher I feel it really is my responsibility to keep something happening in the room. The second is that simply being in a space in which a class-full of faces are often turned towards me heightens my own desire to entertain and perform.

I've heard that in Native American talking circles, people can sit in silence for as long as 20 minutes before they feel a need to speak. But in our culture most groups have great difficulty with such extended silences:

> Psychologists say that a typical group can abide about fifteen seconds of silence before someone feels the need to break the tension by speaking. It is our old friend fear at work, interpreting the silence as something gone wrong, certain that worthwhile things will not happen if we are not making noise.
>
> (Palmer, 1998, p. 77)

Perhaps some part of our fear of silence is natural, like our fear of the dark, but I suspect that our fear of silence, like our fear of the dark, has been abetted by our living in a noisy, brightly lit world, a world that has all but banished true darkness and true silence from our lives. Maybe if we hadn't been brought up in the twentieth century, we would have more patience with silence. I suspect that silence may be even more difficult for students growing up in the twenty-first century.

I recently led a playmaking project at the Atelier at Princeton University. Many of the students in that workshop seemed enormously pressured by their classwork, and they had become so accustomed to filling every moment with activity that every time we took a break from rehearsing, they immediately flipped on their cell phones or opened their laptops to work on homework for other classes. Their nervous energy was so relentless that at one point I asked them to try just sitting silently in a circle for sixty seconds. After fifteen seconds several of them started to talk to each other. It seemed that silence and stillness were simply unbearable for them. Unfortunately in this workshop, I too was feeling time pressure; we were rehearsing a play due to open in a couple of weeks, so I didn't stop our process—as I might have in another situation—to allow these students to examine what it was that happened to them when they faced silence. But this experience did remind me that while I'm trying to help my students expand and deepen their art-making experience, these same students may be under enormous pressure in the rest of their lives pushing them in a very different direction.

Learning in (and from) silence

As I suggested in the chapter on Listening, silence can speak volumes about what is happening in a class—if we are able to pay attention to it.

But paying attention to silence, attending to emptiness rather than rushing in to fill it, can take a great deal of practice and patience for those of us—both students and teachers—who are accustomed to filling the dead air.

Thomas Kasulis suggests that one way for a teacher to move a class in that direction is for a teacher to become

> cognizant of subtle signs of a student's desire to participate—a look in the eye or a shifting in the seat, perhaps. Sometimes in such cases the teacher's glance in the student's direction is enough encouragement so that the hand will go up.
>
> (Kasulis, 1982, p. 42)

Parker Palmer goes one step further:

> Sometimes I use a simple rule that allows these silences to occur naturally instead of requiring my intervention. I merely ask that a student not speak more than twice (or three times in an emergency) in the course of an hour's conversation. The results are quite remarkable. Because of the pauses, the slowed pace, many more people speak than do in the normal free-for-all discussion. The more aggressive and verbal students (the twenty percent who usually dominate eighty percent of the talk) are checked and reined. They are forced to sort and sift what they have to say, looking for that which is essential. The quieter, more retiring students suddenly find the space to speak.
>
> (Palmer, 1983, pp. 80–81)

Richard Fraher, however, another teacher who has wrestled with this question, wonders whether Palmer is right when he suggests that the "quieter, more retiring students" always desire a "space to speak":

> Does the reticence of the archetypal "quiet student" convey disinterest in the subject, lack of confidence about speaking out, cynicism about the value of the discussion process, personal distaste for the teacher and peers, or simply disinclination to speak out?
>
> (Fraher, 1982, pp. 122–23)

Searching for an answer to that question, Anne French Dalke, who teaches at Bryn Mawr, asked students in her Gender and Literature classes to compose short essays on the question of speaking and silence in class. Abby Reed, one of the students who had not spoken much, wrote that she experienced the class as an exercise in "competition for limited airtime." Abby complained that "her classmates, who were intent on articulating their own perceptions, did not attend to and did not make space for her own." On the other hand, Dalke says:

> Not all the quiet students in our gender class were envious of those who spoke. ... Some of them argued, conversely, for the right to be—even the virtue of being—silent.
>
> (Dalke, 2002, p. 85)

As one commented:

> Sitting in class the other day, I wondered where was our space for silence, for listening to one another and not just worrying about needing to say something that contributes to class learning. ... I feel that listening can also contribute to class learning. ... I have come to realize after four years of college that saying something just for the sake of having spoken is often more detrimental to learning than saying nothing at all. I want a space in this class to be accepted for listening to others speak and not to feel judged ... that I haven't said enough.
>
> (Dalke, 2002, p. 85)

But other students in the class had a very different response:

> Many quiet students have told me they are grateful that I insist on their speaking; it's a welcome relief, they say, to know that they *must* speak, that I respect them enough to assure them the time and space they need to do so.
>
> (Dalke, 2002, p. 66)

So how is a teacher to satisfy all these conflicting needs? The problem, of course, is that silence is ... silent. It presents the teacher with an apparently blank slate. Nonetheless, Palmer asserts, all students have something to say, and it is our job as teachers to make a space in which they can say it:

> Behind their fearful silence, our students want to find their voices, speak their voices, have their voices heard. A good teacher is one who can listen to those voices even before they are spoken—so that someday they can speak with truth and confidence.
>
> What does it mean to listen to a voice before it is spoken? It means making space for the other, being aware of the other, paying attention to the other, honoring the other. It means not rushing to fill our students' silences with fearful speech of our own and not trying to coerce them into saying the things that we want to hear.
>
> (Palmer, 1998, p. 46)

It may or may not be true that all students "want to find their voices," but certainly Palmer is right when he says that that if we "fill our students' silences with fearful speech of our own," we make it more difficult for them to "have their voices heard." If we wish to empower students to reveal whatever may lie hidden within their silences, we must try to exhibit some silences of our own.

Silence as a teaching tool

The importance of taking time for this sort of "inner work" was manifest in one of the most powerful—and the simplest—lessons that Jerzy Grotowski taught: the Hunker. After every intense physical exercise, Grotowski instructed us to crouch down, with our feet on the ground, head hanging down, and let ourselves really rest.[2] After working hard at an artistic task, and after risking the physical and emotional effort that task required, it was extremely helpful, Grotowski felt, for an actor to take time to digest, to reflect, to remember, and to let things sink in before plunging into self-criticism or any other activity—certainly before beginning small-talk with one's friends.

In fact, this esoteric practice has solid scientific backing. Scientists have found that rats learn best if, after a new experience, they are given a break during which their brains can build a persistent memory of the experience. Also:

> At the University of Michigan, a study found that people learned significantly better after a walk in nature than after a walk in a dense urban environment, suggesting that processing a barrage of information leaves people fatigued.
>
> (Richtel, *New York Times*, August 24, 2010 on line)

In a similar vein, neuroscientist James Zull observes that the time taken for "Reflective Observation" is critical.

> Probably the most obvious point is that we should be careful not to overload working memory. A classic error of college teachers is to keep shoving information in one end of working memory, not realizing that they are shoving other data out the other end.
>
> (Zull, 2002, p. 184)

---

2 After teaching this squatting hunker for a number of years, I realized that this position was uncomfortable for students with short Achilles tendons, so I've taken to suggesting alternatives: The yoga position called "child's pose," or even sitting quietly alone, perhaps writing notes in one's journal.

What is true for students is no less true for teachers. Recently I've become aware that while my students take the time for a hunker after they work, I'm also stealing a few precious moments of healthy silence and stillness for myself. With the help of students like Deirdre—and the Naropa University practice of beginning and ending every class with a moment of silence and a bow—I'm starting to appreciate how unnecessary is the hurry I've always felt as a teacher, the pressure to get the curriculum accomplished as the syllabus promises and to fill each classroom moment with active learning. I've become aware of how difficult it is for me to be quiet and just allow learning to arise on its own.

The compulsion to speak

The focus of this chapter has been upon the importance of giving support for those students who are silent, giving them the time and space they need to express themselves. But Jane Tompkins notes that the other extreme, the students who *always* speak up may also need support, because the compulsive need to speak may be as burdensome to them as the inability to speak is to the silent ones:

> The terrible need to talk and be listened to and the terrible way people feel when someone imposes this need on them are subjects rarely spoken about in a serious way. The need for attention is huge and sometimes seems insatiable, and the need to be free from such impositions is equally strong and desperate.
>
> (Tompkins, 1996, p. 64)

I wonder what I might have learned if, when I was in school, I had had a teacher like Jane Tompkins or Anne Dalke, someone who could have helped me become aware of my compulsion to speak in class.

Recently, even as I've tried to expand the space for silence in my classes, I have also begun to search for ways to help the most talkative students notice what is driving their need to speak. With some, I simply suggest that they try to observe what it is they feel in the fleeting moment before they raise their hands. With others, the ones who seem most desperate for attention, I sometimes try to address that need directly. A few years ago, there was one young man whose hand always shot up to ask one more question right at the very end of class. If I closed the discussion before calling on him, he would approach me as the others were leaving, seeking a response. His questions were often very intelligent, but his need to ask them, it seemed to me, bespoke something else: a bottomless craving for attention and affection. So, one day as he approached me and began to speak, I put my finger to my lips for a moment, and then I stood silently with him, just making eye contact and holding his hands in mine. After a minute or so, tears welled up in his eyes, he smiled, and we parted, wordlessly. I had not responded to the question he had been about to ask, but it felt as though the question behind his question had been answered.

Perhaps the central point here is that in the classroom—or in any social interaction—it is not only the *content* of what we say or leave unsaid that is meaningful. There is also meaning within the *form*: within our need to speak or to remain silent. If we make a space in which our habits in this regard can be examined, then the information, the emotion, and the wisdom hidden within our need to speak or to remain silent can be revealed.

Pacific silence

Before I conclude this chapter, let me recount one last story about silence.

Many years ago, when I was teaching an improv class at NYU, the head of the Experimental Theater Wing told me he'd like to let a visiting San Francisco director lead my class for a day. Sure, I said. The Californian was introduced, and began by asking the students to stand in a circle. After a couple of minutes of standing doing nothing, the students, young actors who'd spent two years training into the energy of New York City, began looking at one another. After a few more minutes of waiting, one of them finally blurted out: "Is that it? Are we just going to stand here for the whole class!?"

"Good!" the West Coast guru answered, "that's very good."

If I remember right, during the next few minutes some of the students sat down, or lay down, or started reading, until the teacher finally suggested another exercise. Ever since, I've wondered if this was a deep and powerful lesson, or a ridiculous waste of time, or both. But I've never forgotten it.

Silent teaching

For teachers who think they might like to explore what more silence might do for their classes, here are a few suggestions from Thomas Kasulis, Parker Palmer, J. T. Dillon, and from me:

- Sit in silence for a minute or two before you begin and/or at the end of an exercise.
- Notice the non-verbal signals of a desire to speak.

- Don't call on the first hand that goes up.
- Pause before responding to a student's question.
- Ask people in a talking circle to wait for fifteen seconds after each person speaks, letting what has been said sink in.
- Stipulate that students not speak more than twice in the course of an hour's discussion.
- Entertain the possibility that the student who asks a question may not need a verbal answer at all; that a look, a smile, or a touch is really what's called for.

If you try any of these, however, note this caution from Parker Palmer:

> In most places where people meet, silence is a threatening experience. It makes us feel self-conscious and awkward; it feels like some kind of failure. So the teacher who uses silence must understand that a silent space seems inhospitable at first to people who measure progress by noise. Silence must be introduced cautiously; we must allow ourselves to be slowly re-formed in its discipline before it can become an effective teaching tool.
>
> (Palmer, 1983, p. 81)

Chapter 14

What are we really teaching?

Good teaching involves reweaving the spirit.

Mary Rose O'Reilley

Several years ago I was invited to teach an acting workshop for a group of graduate students at the National Theater School in Helsinki, Finland. The school is the only graduate acting program in the country, and it admits just 12 students—every other year! So every student in my class was sure she would be able to land a job acting when she graduated. This was the first time I'd ever had the thought: If these students learn something in my class, each one of them will be able to apply what she has learned to actually making a living. How strange, and how delightful.

That isn't how we do things in America. Here we have hundreds of acting programs, undergraduate drama departments, private acting academies, MFA theater programs, workshops, and private teachers, to say nothing of thousands upon thousands of theater classes on the high school level, all filled with young actors many of whom are hoping to make a living—maybe even become famous—as a stage, film, or TV actor. Although many of these young artists will quickly realize that they won't survive in "the business," enough of them do keep at it that Actors' Equity, the stage actors' union, reported in 2011 that the median annual earnings for union members during the 2010–2011 season was $7,382, and that the average number of weeks members were employed during the year was 17 (Actors' Equity, 2011, pp. 4–5). And that's only the union members. It doesn't count the many thousands of others who are not Equity members. In film and TV, the figures are even more depressing: The Screen Actors Guild reports that the average income earned from acting by the 100,000 or so actors who are union members is about $5,000 per year.[1] A great many of those few who *do* make a

---

[1] http://www.jobbankusa.com/career_employment/actors_producers_directors/salary_wages_pay.html. An online article by Jobbank USA.

living at their craft feel that in order to survive they must compromise their talents by making commercials, working on scripts they dislike, or with directors they don't respect.

Among musicians, the statistics are equally bleak: "A survey of over 200 independent musicians, DJs, producers and bands found that … almost a quarter (23%) actually lose money on their musical endeavors, and less than five percent of them made a living."[2] And things are no better for dancers.

We who teach young performers can be quite sure that very few of the students in our classes will ever earn a living using the skills we are teaching them, although of course a few of them will go on performing for years in small, non-profit or community theaters, dance companies and bands, or perhaps they will—irony of ironies—become teachers! All of which leads one to wonder: Why are we spending our lives teaching thousands of students skills they may never use?

The strange thing is, there are actually several good answers to this question.

Transferable skills

First of all, it is worth noting that teachers of many, many subjects are more-or-less in this same boat. The number of students who will spend their lives using their knowledge of geometry or of Civil War history is also vanishingly small.

Second, as I suggested in the Introduction, the information and skills we like to think we are teaching are really only a small part of what we're actually offering our students. As James Wilkinson puts it:

> The causes of the French Revolution, Hamlet's attitude towards his father, the properties of quadratic equations or the function of hemoglobin hold center stage during the course. Yet except for the small number of students destined to become historians, Shakespeare scholars, mathematicians, or biochemists, the lasting value of what is taught is likely to be a general set of mind that remains even when the particulars of the subject matter have become blurred. William James noted the importance of what he termed "transfer of training" – taking skills learned in one context and applying them to another. Such general skills and attitudes are what the student will retain long after most dates, facts and equations have been forgotten or superseded.
> (Wilkinson, 1982, p. 2)

[2] http://www.dizzyjam.com/blog/?p=155. An online blog article by dizzyjam.

Looking back over what I've written, it seems to me that several of the stories I've told have been stories about such "transferable skills": the story of the student who learned to stand by her convictions by refusing to finish the scene from *The Beauty Queen of Leenane*; the story of Cecelia, who understood that she was more afraid of being really good than she was of being bad; and the story of Sandor, who learned the difference between being right and being helpful. (To say nothing of the stories of a teacher who—I hope—is slowly learning to be at peace with his mistakes.)

Thus, in the chapter on Listening, I suggested that all performance skills are also trainings in listening. Certainly the ability to listen well is a skill our students will be able to apply in all kinds of circumstances, no matter what they happen to find themselves doing for a living. Moreover, learning how to listen also means learning Patience—not a bad thing to have acquired in one's education.

Several times in the course of this book, I have recounted the many lessons I teach about the uses of fear. In the chapter on Questions I wrote about the Tiger Leap exercise, which helps students to convert fear directly into courage, and I mentioned Just Stand, an exercise that converts stage fright itself into a source of creative energy. In *A Soprano on her Head*, Eloise Ristad describes how musicians encounter this same lesson:

> Permission. The very word relaxes a spot in my center and lets me take a deep breath. If I can permit myself to feel scared, I can also permit myself to reinterpret the scared feelings as excitement, for excitement and fear come from the same adrenaline. ... The moments when I have felt that interchange between myself and an audience have been special, and they did not come about because I managed to put a lid on my nervousness, but because I used it.
>
> (Ristad, 1982, p. 170)

The meta-lesson here—that what we experience as "fear" is not something that need overwhelm us, but an energy source that can motivate creativity— is, it seems to me, more than just a "transferable skill." It is a life-lesson, which, once learned, can serve us in all kinds of unsettling circumstances. If we teachers of performance taught our students no more than how to transform their fears into positive creative sources, that lesson alone might be worth the tuition.

Of course, exactly which "transferable skills" a teacher imparts will have something to do with: (1) the particular discipline he is teaching, (2) his manner of instruction, and (3) his interest in communicating such extra-curricular ideas. One of the things I have always liked about teaching the kind of acting I do is that it lends itself to just this sort of extra-curriculum. So, inextricably entwined with my lessons in acting are notions as basic as:

- You can live with questions that have no immediate answers.
- You can learn to work alone by discovering the "secure partner" you carry within you, that inner voice that supports you when you face the unknown.
- By learning how to empathize with characters you dislike, and how to view the world from another's point of view, you grow more powerful and more compassionate at the same time.
- Loss is survivable.
- You can remain open in the face of what Hamlet calls "the thousand natural shocks that flesh is heir to."

Beyond such particular skills, all performance disciplines can—if the teacher so desires—help students rediscover the connections between body and mind that they may have lost during their long years of academic education. By supporting our students in their voyage along the *via negativa*, we not only empower their art-making, we also enable them to reintegrate the essential human wholeness that 12 years of sitting in chairs and raising their hands may have dis-integrated.

Meta-lessons

Beyond these "transferable skills," there are other, even larger, ramifications and corollaries to what—and how—we teach. For many of our lessons bespeak deep educational and ethical Values; not values as concepts or commandments, but as practical ways of living and working. Values such as:

- Experimentation: the ability to discover new truths by daring to try something you've never tried before.
- How to balance Safety and Risk-taking.
- How to live in the moment, neither ruing the past nor obsessing about the future.
- The importance of Rule-breaking.
- The ability to "shine, as children do."
- The ability to withstand—perhaps even to enjoy—making mistakes.

No matter what our discipline, we also teach the great lesson of how to train—the lesson contained in the punch line of the joke: "How do

you get to Carnegie Hall?"—"Practice, practice, practice." Not to mention small things like Self-awareness, Self-confidence, and the spiritual
lesson upon which the effectiveness of our teaching itself depends:
loving-kindness.

Perhaps this long list of transferable skills and meta-lessons can
assuage our concern that we might be wasting our time teaching students
skills they will never employ. But that is not really my point. My point
goes back to the very reason I wanted to write this book: that if we
examine this list, we will find that many of these transferable skills and
value-lessons depend less upon *what* we teach than upon *how* we teach it.

For instance, we cannot teach the value of experimentation as a theoretical
lecture. We cannot encourage the revolutionary practice of rule-breaking
while holding students strictly to the rules. If we wish to free our students
from self-judgment, we must find ways to give them feedback that does
not make them feel more judged. If we wish to teach them that making
mistakes can be a joyful process, we must demonstrate an ability to be
equally lighthearted about our own. To conclude: If we really want
our students to live with questions, we must be willing to live with
questions ourselves. Here are some of the ones that presently confound
me—followed by my current, tentative responses.

My questions

How do I take responsibility for what I do as a teacher without blaming myself for those things that are beyond my control?

In several of the stories I've related in this book, I agonize about the
teaching "mistakes" I've made. But meditation teacher Sharon Salzberg
points out that in our lives and in our work, we can take responsibility
for our *intentions,* and we can take responsibility for using *skillful
means* to achieve those intentions, but we cannot take responsibility for
the results. So, in our teaching, for example, we can keep in mind that
our job as teachers is to be helpful, and we can take care to notice how
counter-transference is affecting our reactions to a student, but even
doing both of those things does not insure that we will be able to help
every student learn what we are trying to teach, for our students' lives
are subject to many other events over which we have no control.
Therefore, even with all the best intentions and all the skillful means we
can muster, the *outcomes* of our actions remain beyond our control.
The problem, Salzberg suggests, is that we often judge ourselves not by
those things we can control—the intentions and the means—but by the
results. As Anne Bogart puts it: "You cannot create results; you can

only create the conditions in which something might happen" (Bogart, 2001, p. 124).

For whom do we make art? For ourselves or for our audiences? And does our answer to this question have implications for how we teach?

Terrance Keenan tells this story about a childhood conversation he had while sitting for his grandfather who was a painter:

> At some point the story [that my grandfather was telling] petered out or he become absorbed in some problem on the canvas. Things grew quiet. I could hear the old mahogany grandmother clock, brought over from Ireland and called that because it was smaller than a grand *father* clock, ticking loudly and slowly downstairs. "Granpop?" I asked suddenly, "Why do you paint?" He paused, brush in hand, a dark lock over his brow. His eyes, often bleary, became very, very clear and looked at me as though he had never seen me before. "Well, my boy," he said, "Art is my way to talk to God."
>
> (Keenan, 2001, p. 33–34)

But painting is a solitary activity, one that can easily be performed without an earthly audience; acting and music and dance performances require human witnesses. Don't they?

I once attended a concert by a violinist who played a very strange, hard-to-listen-to modern composition. After the piece was finished, there was time for questions and answers, and one young person in the audience had the temerity to ask, "How would you feel if the audience walked out while you were playing?"

"It wouldn't matter to me at all," the violinist replied, "I'm playing for myself."

Bertolt Brecht, on the other hand, felt that the central purpose of art was to motivate the audience to think and to act: "Art is not a mirror held up to reality," he said, "but a hammer with which to shape it."

So I wonder, do performing artists play for themselves or do they perform to affect their audiences? Grotowski believed that Brecht was right only if the violinist was also right. He felt that a performer is able to transform his audience only when he is striving to transform himself:

> Why do we sacrifice so much energy to our art? Not in order to teach others but to learn with them what our existence, our organism, our personal and unrepeatable experience have to give us; to learn to

break down the barriers which surround us and to free ourselves from ... the lies about ourselves which we manufacture daily for ourselves and for others; to destroy the limitations caused by our ignorance and lack of courage; in short, to fill the emptiness in our soul. ... We see theatre – especially in its palpable, carnal aspect – as a place of provocation, a challenge the actor sets himself and also, indirectly, other people.

(Grotowski, 1976, p. 212)

My personal opinion is that the joy of performance is an interactive one. It is a joy that arises from the act of giving a gift, and that act requires both a giver and a receiver.

The same, it seems to me, holds true of teaching. That is why the act of Listening is so essential to both performance and teaching, for both—to use Grotowski's words—depend upon "the attitude of giving and receiving which springs from true love: in other words self-sacrifice" (Grotowski, 1976, p. 35). But "giving and receiving" implies a dialogue, not a lecture, a generosity and an empathy for one's audience, not an attitude of "Look at how impressive and difficult-to-understand this piece is." That is why I admire the kind of art—and the kind of teaching—that demystifies even as it impresses.

The "painterly" work of Maurice de Vlaminck, for instance, invites the viewer to discern both the image *and* the artist's brush-stroke at the same time. By making his brush-strokes obvious, Vlaminck reveals the secret behind the illusion, thus inviting all his viewers to be artists too.

I once saw a production of Yevgeny Schwartz's play *The Dragon* in East Berlin, which demystified stage-magic in a similar way. A character on stage had suddenly to become invisible. To accomplish this trick, the actor simply stood stock-still in the middle of the stage while a long burlap cloth quickly descended from above. A moment later the cloth flew back up, and the actor was gone. It was obvious that a trap had opened on stage through which the actor had fallen, and yet the disappearance was magical. The whole audience was in on the trick but utterly entranced.

The artist who lets you in on his process is like a magician who can impress you with a magic trick even while he explains to you how he is doing it. Such a magician allows you to feel that magic is something that you, too, could do.

However, the teacher who wishes to share his magic with his students faces the consequences of neoteny I mentioned in the chapter on Power and Control: the students' propensity to regard their teachers as holders of secret powers and wisdom. I know that when I watched Jerzy Grotowski teaching, I sometimes sat there in awe, mystified by the "magic" he was doing. What, I wondered, was he seeing that I could not see, and how did he choose what to say to each student? For, though Grotowski was very clear in his instructions to actors, he never explained what he was doing as a teacher. It took me years to shake off my awe and to realize that what Grotowski had been doing was not magic, but rather a kind of physical empathy—combined, perhaps, with a rather uncompromising, Polish version of what Buddhists call Loving-kindness.

The central purpose of education, I believe, is to help our students become their own teachers, so I think that a part of my job is to undermine any dependency or awe they may experience by trying to demystify the work I am doing as I do it. That is why I try to help students see what I am seeing and understand how I am working. Often, after working with one actor, I will remind the class that what I did was simply reinforce a piece of feedback the actor had already given himself; and after seeing a powerful physical choice I had pointed to blossom as a student works on a monologue, I will point out to the class that all of us had seen the seed of that gesture in miniature the first time she went through her text.

So my admiration for performers who listen to their audiences and for art that demystifies is reflected in my dedication to a pedagogy that also exemplifies listening and demystification.

These are just *my* opinions. The essential point I'm trying to make here is: The way we answer the question, "Do we make art for ourselves or for our audiences" does, indeed, have implications for how we teach. It is, therefore, a worthwhile question for teachers to ask themselves.

What kinds of performance does the world need now? And does our answer to that question also have consequences for the kind of teaching we do?

In 1957, Thornton Wilder published an anthology of his plays, *Our Town*, *The Skin of our Teeth*, and *The Matchmaker*. In the preface to that anthology, he explains that he began to write plays because he was dissatisfied with the kind of theater he saw, theater that had been invented during the nineteenth century "to be *soothing*," and to satisfy and pacify audiences who were "assured of eternal life in the next world, and, in this, [one] ... squarely seated on Property and the privileges that accompany it" (Wilder, 1957, p. xxvii).

In the nineteenth century, alcohol and opium were the drugs of choice, and religion, as Karl Marx noted, served as "the opium of the people." Similarly, the theater of the time, Wilder writes, was designed to help its audiences avoid asking the "questions that must not be asked." Questions about the meaning of life, about power, and about what Wilder calls the "wide tracts of injustice and stupidity in the world." So he purposefully wrote plays that provoked audiences to ask the "questions that must not be asked."

Wilder was not alone. Throughout much of the twentieth century, artists in every medium strove to make work that was not soothing, art that riled, galled, offended, or incited audiences. Artists like Bertolt Brecht, Harold Pinter, Carol Churchill, John Cage, John Lennon, Stanley Kubrick, Tom Waits, Marcel Duchamp, and Diane Arbus—and many more—all created art that pushed audiences to ask some of those "questions that must not be asked." In fact one might say that what makes the most striking art of the twentieth century so striking is that it is *not* soothing.

The problem is that the problem has changed. It is no longer true that our culture seeks to pacify us by *soothing* us. Instead, the culture of the twenty-first century attempts to *distract* us from the "wide tracts of injustice and stupidity in the world." Nowadays the juggernaut of our economy depends upon each of us not having time to consider what we are buying, whom we are working for, or what the consequences of our activities might be. Instead of opioids, the fashionable intoxicants of our era are caffeine and cocaine, and nowadays our mega-churches and televangelism promote a religion that we might call "the amphetamine of the people." Similarly, rather than lulling us to sleep, our twenty-first century culture inundates us with input and fascinates our minds with multi-tasking, leaving us with neither the time nor the mental clarity to focus upon those "questions that must not be asked."

So, while Thornton Wilder felt that the task of concerned artists in the twentieth century was to create art that could awaken audiences who had been lulled into complacency, twenty-first century artists must figure out how to make work that can liberate audiences from overload, simultaneity, and distraction. But how do we do that? What kind of art can attract the attention of a distracted audience without itself becoming one more distraction? How does one "awaken" an audience that is chronically hyper-awake?

I don't know. But every once in a while, I witness some work in my classes that hints at an answer to this question.

Almost every year, at some point, the open warm-up time in my acting classes becomes extremely loud. Many small groups of students get lost in exploring their own little dances, rhythms, and scenelets, and the air in the studio becomes filled with a cacophony of simultaneous screams and laughs and groans. Most of the students are not bothered by the noise, but often enough there is one student who feels terribly oppressed by the sounds that fill the air.

"It's so loud I can't think," she complains to me. "And I feel trapped because if I just yell 'Shut up,' I've got to be even louder than everyone else." Her point is well taken. (In fact, it speaks to the classic problem of revolutionists: If the rebels must use the tactics of the oppressors in order to change their circumstances, don't they, themselves, become the new oppressors?)

If there is a solution to this conundrum, it requires an ability to see (or hear) the problem in a new way. One year, for instance, a student who craved silence at such a moment discovered that if she simply raised her index finger to her lips and quietly went around the room saying, "Shh" to each group, the clarity and power of this little gesture and this particular sound easily cut through the uproar.

At other times, I've found that the noisy students themselves can transform their cacophony into harmony without needing to inhibit their creative energy—*if* they can apply what they have learned about Listening. If I remind them to extend their peripheral vision and to listen to what is happening in the whole room, they can begin to hear that the "noise" that is filling the space is actually made up of myriad rhythms and pitches, rhythms and pitches into which they can fit the sounds they themselves are making. They discover that this is not difficult because the human mind is actually designed to find patterns within disorder and to perceive unity within complexity. Thus harmony can arise directly out of cacophony, if we know how to listen for it.

And is this not exactly the way that harmony works in music?

Unlike multi-tasking or channel-surfing, harmony neither overloads or fatigues our minds. Instead it transforms simultaneous and diverse inputs directly into serenity. It accomplishes this alchemy by focusing our awareness not upon the separate notes of a chord but rather on the space *between* those notes—on the vibrational interference pattern that exists precisely because the notes are dissimilar. In other words, the peculiar power of harmony derives from the mind's innate ability to perceive the Concord that exists within Difference and the Unity that arises from Diversity.

Although this process is most obvious in music, it can be seen in other art forms too. Magritte's paintings, Kurosawa's *Rashomon*, Kubrick's *2001*, Pirandello's *Six Characters in Search of an Author*, and John Patrick Stanley's *Doubt* all derive their power by opening us to the beauty that resides within Difference, Contradiction, Paradox, and Uncertainty.

Do these twentieth century works point toward the kind of art the twenty-first century needs? If so, is the ability to Listen—deeply and constantly—the most important skill we can offer to students who must discover how to make the kind of art that could lead today's jaded and overloaded audiences to "ask the questions that must not be asked"?

What does our teaching have to do with our politics?

Most of the teachers I know think of themselves as political liberals; some—myself included—might consider themselves even further to the Left. But I sometimes wonder if our politics are at odds with our attitudes toward teaching.

As I suggested in the first chapter of this book, we are all born with a great natural capacity for Wonder, but step-by-step that capacity often becomes corroded by our experiences in this world. As our Wonder matures it becomes the act of Questioning, but open-ended Questioning necessitates an ability to live with uncertainty, and if our Questioning devolves into a need to have answers, it loses contact with its Wondrous roots. The expectation that answers can save us from uncertainty is the very mainspring of fundamentalism. As the Fundamentalist Preacher in *The Laramie Project* says, "The Word is either sufficient, or it is not."

The political and social consequences of such fundamentalist thinking are currently playing havoc with the world we live in, and artists in many countries have felt the sting of this absolutist outlook. Creativity demands openness, risk-taking, and incompleteness—values entirely opposite to those of fundamentalism.

Education theorist David Kolb puts it this way:

> The greatest challenge to the development of knowledge is the comfort of dogmatism—the security provided by unquestioned confidence in a statement of truth, or in a method for achieving truth.
>
> (Kolb, 1984, p. 108)

After writing this, Kolb goes one step further; he asserts that at the opposite extreme, skepticism is itself a kind of "shadow dogmatism." "To be utterly skeptical," he writes, "is to dogmatically affirm that nothing can be known."

It seems to me that this utter Skepticism is nothing more than our original Wonder now soured by our encounters with the frustrations of this world. Once we Wondered about the things we did not comprehend. Then we Questioned how they came to be. Now we have become Skeptical that anything that seems incomprehensible is real. This mental corrosion process leads to one final stage: out-and-out Cynicism. Who among us is entirely immune to this moral oxidation? Parker Palmer writes:

It is not unusual to see faculty in midcareer don the armor of cynicism against students, education, and any sign of hope. It is the cynicism that comes when the high hopes one once had for teaching have been dashed by experience—or by the failure to interpret one's experience accurately.

(Palmer, 1998, p. 48)

Grotowski warned actors against donning just such armor: "A very 'armed' actor," he told us, "is often a very insecure one. Resign yourself, from being armed, from knowing what to do. Face yourself as though unknown" (Crawley, 1978, p. XIII-10).

If in order to make art, an artist must "resign" himself from being armed, what of the artist's teacher? Is it not equally necessary for us, as exemplars, to resign ourselves from being armed? How are we to exhort our students towards Wonder and real Questioning if we ourselves become cynical?

My personal fears run in the opposite direction.

In the 1960s, when many bumper stickers read: "Question Authority," I certainly did so, with vehemence and determination, but also with enthusiasm and hope. Nowadays, however—after 40 years of mendacious politicians, military adventurism, avaricious financiers, and reality TV—my Questioning of Authority has, I fear, lost touch with its Wondrous ancestry and has become burdened with exactly the sort of Cynicism I try so hard to avoid when facing my students.

Unlike those teachers who Parker Palmer says "don the armor of cynicism against students," I think that my pedagogy has, for the most part, continued to convey my belief in the necessity for Wonder. But I'm afraid that my attitude toward the world has failed to appreciate the lessons I try so hard to teach. When I'm teaching, I sometimes point out to my students how the lessons they are learning in our acting class—about the importance of Listening or the uses of Fear, for instance—can serve them in other aspects of their lives. Now I wonder why I have such a hard time applying the lessons I teach about Wonder and Questioning to my own life. Would that my politics could take a lesson from my teaching! As Albert Einstein said:

The most beautiful experience we can have is the mysterious. It is the fundamental emotion which stands at the cradle of true art and true science. Whoever does not know it and can no longer wonder, no longer marvel, is as good as dead, and his eyes are dimmed.

(Einstein, 1954, pp. 193–94)

An afterword about grading

While I was teaching at the NYU Tisch School of the Arts, I served for two years as a member, and then as chair, of the Dean's Committee on Academic Affairs. The committee met on the top floor of the building at 721 Broadway, the floor with all the Deans' offices and with a large meeting room for full faculty meetings, a room with a commanding view towards the west across Manhattan.

One Tuesday morning in September, 2001, I showed up early for our first committee meeting, so I had time to stare out those windows before our meeting started. The sky was wonderfully clear and bright, and as I looked out the window, I noticed an airplane flying south over Manhattan. "That's strange," I thought, "that plane is flying very low." Then I left the meeting room and went into the Dean's office for our meeting.

Since it was the first meeting of our committee, the Dean spent time explaining to us just what the regular responsibilities of the Committee on Academic Affairs were; he said that our usual job would be to review proposals for new courses that faculty members had sent to the Dean for approval. During the following year, he also asked us to investigate just how the faculty in the Tisch School of the Arts approached their least favorite task: grading their students. To do so we would poll the faculty with questionnaires, we would gather data, and then we would make recommendations. Along the way, we learned how terribly knotty the issue of grading is, and what an overwhelming task it can be to change the entrenched habits of hundreds of faculty, each of whom has his or her own idea of what this unpleasant task is all about.

Toward the end of that first meeting of our committee, one of the administrative assistants interrupted the meeting to tell us that something strange was happening one mile downtown at the World Trade Center. At the end of the meeting, I took the elevator down to the street level and walked across Waverly Place and through Washington Square towards my home. When I got close to the Washington arch I could see, one mile to the south, both towers of the World Trade Center in flames. While we had been sitting talking calmly about "academic affairs," a mile away the world had changed.

Really, it did not require such a catastrophe to sense the utter inconsequence of our committee's efforts. The following year, as we delved into the grading situation at our school, we soon learned the Sisyphean nature of the task we faced. We learned that marking systems varied widely from department to department, and within departments, from teacher to teacher. We found that some teachers considered "C" an acceptable grade while others gave automatic "A"s to students who showed up in class. Some teachers said they took "talent" into consideration when grading, others told us their grades were based upon "improvement," or upon the "completion of assigned work" while still others said "effort" was their paramount criterion, though within that cohort, different faculty members had very different ideas about just what "effort" meant. Some teachers said they graded "on a curve," while several considered grading on a curve unethical and inappropriate in a creative field and one faculty member wrote to the committee that he had no idea what "grading on a curve" meant.[1] Some thought all courses should be Pass/Fail, some thought that wouldn't work because it would make it harder for some students to get scholarships or to be admitted to graduate programs. As I mentioned in the chapter on Power and Control, some part-time faculty were afraid of giving low grades because they thought it might lead students to write negative comments on their faculty evaluations and feared that those negative evaluations would endanger their jobs—and so it went.

What a miasma! The sky was falling, and we were knocking our heads against a wall.

Perhaps the fact that different teachers had very different relationships to grades and grading should not have been a surprise to me. I'd first become aware of that fact back in 1976, when my wife Suzanne and I were both asked to teach at Emerson College. It had been a big deal for us. I'd been teaching for three years at The Acting Growth Program that Linda Putnam and I had started. The Program had been a success, which meant that Linda and I were now earning upwards of $150 a week (for 30 weeks) each year. But Emerson said they were going to

---

1 Grading on a curve means distributing the grades in a class so that, no matter how well— or poorly—students do, a certain percentage of the class will receive As, Bs, and Cs. Most curved grading systems use a "bell curve," and assign the majority of the students a middling grade like a B, with fewer students granted As or Cs.

pay me $12,000! So, in spite of the obligatory feelings of guilt, I took the job.

The fall semester at Emerson went well enough. It was a small school, but many of the students had come there specifically to study acting, and the department chairman seemed happy enough with my unconventional approach to actor training. But then, suddenly, as the semester came to an end, Suzanne and I were faced with a task we'd never thought about: Emerson expected us to give our students letter grades, A through F. At the Acting Growth Program we'd had lots and lots of "processing" and face-to-face big-group and small-group feedback. But grades? Certainly not. We were, after all, the counter-culture, and grades were one of the things we were countering.

At Emerson, there was no way around it. It was in the contract: You must grade your students. Luckily, I thought, I could talk this problem through with my wife who was teaching movement to some of the same students; but as she and I began to compare our thoughts on the subject, I got my first inkling of just how fraught this grading business could be with the weight of personal history.

When I'd been a student in high school and college, with very few exceptions, I'd always received As and Bs. That's who I was. During the first semester of my sophomore year of high school, having just transferred from a "progressive" private school to the Bronx High School of Science, my English teacher gave me a C. It was a terrible shock. I was ashamed to show the report card to my parents, and I promised myself it would never happen again.

So when I started teaching at Emerson, and had to hand out grades, I gave everyone As and Bs. To my mind, Cs were a mark reserved for those few students who deserved to feel as terrible as I had when I'd received one.

For Suzanne on the other hand, C had been a grade she'd seen lots of as a student. So when it came time for her to grade her students—many of the same ones I was teaching—she doled out several Cs as a matter of course. Her As, on the other hand, were reserved for the very few. It wasn't that our basic criteria were different; both of us believed in grading mostly for "effort" rather than for "talent" or "accomplishment." It was just that we spoke different grading languages. If I gave someone a B it meant "adequate effort, nothing special." But if one of Suzanne's students received a B, it was a compliment. So it should not have surprised me to learn, 25 years later, that every faculty member at the Tisch School of the Arts had his own take on what those letter grades signified.

In 2002, while our Academic Affairs committee gathered data from the faculty, we asked the Dean of Students to query the students on the subject of grading. After collating the results, the Dean reported to us that many of them felt that grading was inconsistent. We were not astonished.

More disheartening was the information we received from one department that, when they had tried to enforce a uniform grading policy within their department, one of the senior faculty members—a Professor who had tenure—had responded that he'd always given As and he wasn't about to change his system now.

Some teachers told us that they thought of their syllabus as a contract that clearly laid out the basis on which students would be graded in that class. Some used "rubrics" to clarify the categories that they would consider when grading students—20 percent for classroom participation, 50 percent for quizzes, etc.—and some began their semesters with discussions at which the students could describe on what basis they thought they should be graded. Many of the systems seemed to make good sense, but each one was a world unto itself.

During the semester we'd also read several academic studies on the subject of grading at schools all across the US, and we'd learned that NYU was not alone in these contradictions. The literature on grading was filled with examples that illustrated the fact that grades don't really mean anything, or rather that they can mean anything at all, depending on the teacher's state of mind. This, for instance, is from a study of teaching methods called *The University Teacher as Artist*:

> Powell [a student] deserved an A but was not given one by Professor Harrison, while Morton [another student] did not deserve an A but was given one by Professor Kaye. Both professors exercised virtually absolute power in grading and used that power in the service of entirely different principles. Powell was not given an A because Professor Harrison believed that college study should be hard work and Powell had not worked hard. Morton received an A because Professor Kaye was convinced that a professor could (and occasionally should), with conscious intent, use grades not to symbolize the quality of the student's past accomplishment but to encourage the student in his future efforts.
>
> (Axelrod, 1973, p. 191)

In her book, *The Peaceable Classroom*, Mary Rose O'Reilley points out how even international politics affected grading at her school:

> What skewed our perception of the moral world of college teaching—was Vietnam. ... We began to change our methods because the

methods by which we ourselves had learned did not work for open admissions students, and we did not want our students, as a consequence of our inept pedagogy, to be killed. We began to see that grading is at least metaphorically a violent act, because in 1967, it was *literally* a violent act.

(O'Reilley, 1993, pp. 8–9)

Perhaps most disheartening were the articles that argued that no matter what grading system a teacher uses, different students will take different lessons from identical grades, depending on their own previous schooling experiences. No matter how clearly a teacher tries to explain her grading method to her class, each student, the article averred, will read the grades he receives through glasses tinted and ground by the hundreds of teachers with whom that student had studied before.

The waters our committee was swimming through seemed hopelessly murky, and yet a couple of basic suggestions floated to the surface:

- In spite of the extra effort involved, most faculty members agreed that it was much more meaningful to give students written and/or verbal evaluations than to depend on grades to provide meaningful feedback.
- Whatever system a teacher employed in determining a grade, she must tell students, in the syllabus or on the very first day in class, exactly what the basis of their grade would be. Not just the percentage based on attendance, on class participation and so on, but the "learning goals" and "outcomes" the teacher has in mind, so that at the end of the semester, the student and the teacher could agree as to whether those goals have been achieved.

This last idea seemed to insure that a teacher could not grade a student on the basis of something he didn't know he was supposed to be working on. It seemed to make a lot of sense. But after our committee made its report to the deans and the departments, I began to wonder if this "goals" and "outcomes" business would really work in my own classes. And the more I thought about it, the more it seemed to me that this seemingly straightforward and demystifying approach might actually undermine my teaching.

Certainly one of the principal "goals" of my teaching was that, little by little, the students should gain insight into their own work processes, that over time they should learn to "see themselves" more and more clearly as they create. But if I were to tell my students on the first day of class that this was the "goal," of their work, wouldn't this "goal" distract them from the daily tasks that lead up to that goal? If, when they were first working on a scene, they were concerned that their grade depended on whether or not they had "insight into their own work processes," wouldn't the scene-work and the insight both suffer? It would be like asking a mountain climber to keep his eyes on the top of the mountain rather than encouraging him to concentrate upon the rock-face he is touching.

Wendell Beavers, the Chair of the MFA in Contemporary Performance Department at Naropa University puts it this way:

> My "pedagogical" strategies, my tactics, goals and driving values, are secret. Yes secret! The legal language I suppose is "proprietary." Especially from my students who, if I told them, would be distracted and undermined in their own very, very difficult, tedious, journey to uncover their own reasons for doing things, for making the effort, for somehow summoning the outrageous courage to hold the space for others to discover themselves with all the terrors and transcendent possibilities that holds. These things are secret because I don't want to rob you of ownership of your own means—to rob you of a "teacher" identity which is as unique as a fingerprint.
>
> (Beavers, 2011)

Moreover, in the process of the *via negativa,* some of the goals keep changing. In fact one might even say that a central "goal" of the work is to allow the goals to change. Many students, for instance, enter my acting classes aiming to integrate the physical approach to acting with their earlier training—a reasonable enough expectation. For some, that is exactly what they accomplish. Along the way, others discover that what is more essential for them at this particular point is that they rediscover the enjoyment that performance once held for them. That goal—one that neither they nor I had been aware of when they started—quite overshadows the one they'd thought they needed to achieve. Then, too, there are some students who enter the training with a clear "outcome" in mind: to prepare a monologue with which to audition. But along the way they realize that acting is not really what they thought it was, and they decide they're going to change their major. Should a student who uses the work to reach such a life-altering insight receive a lower—or a higher—grade than the student who simply accomplished exactly what he set out to do? Thus, although this "goals" and "outcomes" business might give a teacher—or an administrator—some sense of whether or not a course is accomplishing what it was designed to accomplish, I remain doubtful that it does much toward clarifying the overdetermined nature of grading for the student.

In all my years of teaching, I can remember only one time when I felt that giving a grade to a student really made a clear and important difference. One year I had a young man in my acting class who was clearly a very smart guy and a very good actor. But he was also someone for whom everything seemed to come easily—too easily. He'd never had to work hard to do well in school, so he didn't work hard at his acting either. He didn't learn his lines, he didn't rehearse enough. Sometimes he didn't even show up to class on time. At the middle of the semester, I called him into my office to talk. The conversation was going nowhere until I told him that at that point, in mid-semester, he was failing the class. This was a young man who had never been in danger of failing anything in his life. He was clearly stunned by what I'd said. During the last weeks of the class, he was sharp; he worked hard and did some exciting acting. Maybe the same change would have occurred without the threat of a failing grade, but for this particular student, just mentioning the grade seemed to be exactly kind of push that helped. Of course, even in this case, it was the threat that had the effect, not the grade itself, for I never did have to give him that F.

The trouble is that grading—any kind of grading—reinforces two dubious ideas. One is the power issue we've already talked about: Any grade a teacher hands out is a reiteration of the old power relationship between teacher and student. As such, it reinforces the very sort of dependency and passivity that education should serve to undo. Jakovljevic, Hollingshaus, and Foster put it this way:

> The main source of student passivity and disengagement is not the lecture format, and not even the overcrowded classroom. The core problem is in the students' status. Namely, students are not only learners, but also purchasers of skills and of degrees. They are customers. What is passive in the classroom is not a student, but a customer. There is a widespread idea of a customer's agency: a buyer in the free market has the right to choose. Even some of my brightest students thought of themselves as customers. That, they said, gave them a sense of empowerment. This contamination of learning with consumerism creates several dire problems. The most alarming are: the customer does not participate in production, only in consumption; the customer has the right to try out, test, and change, but never to fail; the customer purchases to own, not to share; the customer does not know renunciation; and finally and most alarmingly, the customer does not have the right not to choose.
>
> (Jakovljevic, Hollingshaus, & Foster, 2008, p. 78)

The second mistaken idea that grading promulgates is the assumption that we all know what "failure" means. As I wrote in the chapter "No Mistakes," I think the whole idea of failure is thoroughly misunderstood in our culture, so whatever you—or the student—may think an F means, giving someone this grade also reinforces a false conception of human learning and discovery.

So, even after years of dutifully handing out grades, I remain a bit stumped by the whole subject. For many years, while teaching at NYU where we were required to dispense grades A through F, I thought that perhaps Pass/Fail grading would make more sense, but now that I've taught for several years in a graduate department that does grade Pass/Fail, it's become clear to me that that system has problems too. If, in practice, Pass/Fail really means "everybody passes," then the grade becomes meaningless, so why bother? And if, on the other hand, all those who seem slack in their work will really be failed, the program must provide a way for all of those students—if they wish—to take the class over again.

Personally, I find individual meetings with each student provide a much more meaningful form of evaluation, for they offer a space in which I can adjust my feedback as I see how it is being taken. My hope is that in my classes and in my private meetings with students, I have offered them sufficient feedback and enough warm words of encouragement to counterbalance the inescapable coldness of the grade I must hand out.

Any way you dice it, grades classify students in relation to other students. In doing so they proclaim the power of the teachers and of the institution over the students. And that, it seems to me, is opposite to the very purpose of education: empowering students.

Bibliography

Actors' Equity (2011) 2010–2011 "Theatrical Season Report," http://www. actorsequity.org/docs/about/AEA_Annual_2010-11.pdf Online. Accessed July 23, 2012.

Axelrod, Joseph (1973) *The University Teacher as Artist*, Jossey-Bass Publishers, SF.

Baiocco, Sharon and Jamie N. DeWaters (1998) *Successful College Teaching, Problem-solving Strategies of Distinguished Professors*, Allyn and Bacon, Needham Heights, MA.

Baxtresser, Jeanne (2010) Personal communication.

Beavers, Wendell (2011) Unpublished speech to MFA students, Naropa University, CO.

Beckett, Samuel (1958) *Endgame*, Grove Press, NY.

Belenky, Mary Field, et al. (1986) "Connected Teaching," *Women's Ways of Knowing*, Basic, NY.

Bogart, Anne (2001) *A Director Prepares, Seven Essays on Art and Theatre*, Routledge, London.

——(2010) "Seeing and Doing," *Anne's Blog*, http://siti.groupsite.com/.Online. Accessed September 1, 2010

Chekhov, Michael (1953) *To The Actor, on the Technique of Acting*, Harper and Brothers, NY.

Christensen, C. Roland (1982) Introduction, in Gullette, Margaret Morganroth (ed.) *The Art and Craft of Teaching*, Harvard-Danforth Center for Teaching and Learning, Cambridge, MA.

Crawley, Tom (1978) *The Stone in the Soup* (unpublished manuscript)

Dalke, Anne French (2002) *Teaching to Learn/Learning to Teach, Meditations on the Classroom*, Peter Lang, NY.

Dillon, J. T. (1981) "To Question and not to Question During Discussion," *Journal of Teacher Education*, 32 (6): 15–20.

Dizzyjam (2010) http://www.dizzyjam.com/blog/?p=155. Online. Accessed July 8, 2010.

Edwards, Sandra and Mary Anne Bowman (1996) "Promoting Student Learning Through Questioning: A Study of Classroom Questions," *Journal on Excellence in College Teaching*, 7 (2): 3–24.

Einstein, Albert (1954) *Ideas and Opinions*, tr. Sonja Bargmann, Bonanza Books, Crown Publishers, NY ("What I Believe" originally published in *Forum and Century*, XCVN (3), March 1936).

Elbow, Peter (1986) *Embracing Contraries, Explorations in Learning and Teaching*, New York, Oxford University Press (Chapter: "The Pedagogy of the Bamboozled" first published in *Soundings*, 56 (2), Summer, 1973).

Fish, Stanley (2010) http://opinionator.blogs.nytimes.com/2010/06/21/deep-in-the-heart-of-texas/?scp=1&sq=stanley%20fish,%20texas,%20evaluations&st=cs. Online. Accessed June 21, 2010.

Fiumara, Gemma Corradi (1990) *The Other Side of Language: A Philosophy of Listening*, tr. Charles Lambert, Routledge, NY.

Fordham, S. and J. Ogbu (1986) "Black Student's School Success: Coping with the Burden of 'Acting White,'" *Urban Review*, 18: pp. 176–206.

Fox, Helen (2001) *When Race Breaks Out, Conversations about Race and Racism in College Classrooms*, Peter Lang, NY.

Fraher, Richard (1982) "Learning a New Art: Suggestions for Beginning Teachers," in Margaret Morganroth Gullette (ed.) *The Art and Craft of Teaching*, Harvard-Danforth Center for Teaching and Learning, Cambridge, MA (pp. 116–127).

Freire, Paulo (1970) *Pedagogy of the Oppressed*, tr. Myra Bergman Ramos, Continuum, NY (1999 edition).

Freud, Sigmund (1956–74) *The Complete Psychological Works of Sigmund Freud*, translated from the German under the general editorship of James Stracey, The Hogarth Press and the Institute of Psychoanalysis, London.

Gall, M.D (1970) "The Use of Questions in Teaching," *Review of Educational Research, 40*: 707–720.

Goleman, Daniel (1995) *Emotional Intelligence*, Bantam, NY.

Gopnik, Alison (2010) "How Babies Think," *Scientific American, 303* (1): 76–81, July.

Grambs, Jean Dresden (1972) "Negro Self-Concept Reappraised," in James A. Banks and Jean Dresden Grambs (eds.) *Black Self-Concept, Implications for Education and Social Science*, McGrew-Hill Book Co., NY (pp. 171–220).

Grotowski, Jerzy (1976) *Towards a Poor Theatre* (ed. Eugenio Barba), Methuen, London.

Hagen, Uta (1991) *A Challenge for the Actor*, Scribner, NY.

hooks, bell (1994) *Teaching to Transgress, Education as the Practice of Freedom*, Routledge, NY.

Jakovljevic, Branislav, Wade Hollingshaus, and Mark Foster (2008) "Financialization of Education," *Theatre Topics*, 18 (1): 69–85, *Project Muse, Scholarly journals online*.

Jobbank USA (n.d.) http://www.jobbankusa.com/career_employment/actors_producers_directors/salary_wages_pay.html. Online. Accessed July 23, 2012.

Kasulis, Thomas P. (1982) "Questioning," in Margaret Morganroth Gullette (ed.) *The Art and Craft of Teaching*, Harvard-Danforth Center for Teaching and Learning, Cambridge, MA (pp. 38–48).

Keenan, Terrance (2001) *St. Nadie in Winter, Zen Encounters with Loneliness*, Journey Editions, Boston, MA.

Kohl, Herbert (1994) *"I Won't Learn from You" and Other Thoughts on Creative Maladjustment*, The New Press, NY.

Kolb, David A. (1984) *Experiential Learning, Experience as the Source of Learning and Development*, Prentice Hall, Inc. Englewood Cliffs, NJ.

Krantz, James (1999) "Comment on Challenging Resistance to Change," *Journal of Behavioral and Applied Science*, 35 (1): 42–44, March.

Light, Greg and Roy Cox (2001) *Learning and Teaching in Higher Education, the Reflective Professional*, Paul Chapman Publishing, London.

McCourt, Frank (2005) *Teacher Man, a Memoir*, Scribner, NY.

McDonagh, Martin (1996) *The Beauty Queen of Leenane*, Methuen, London.

McGrane, Bernard (1998) Personal interview.

Meisner, Sanford and and Dennis Longwell (1987) *Sanford Meisner on Acting*, Vintage, NY.

Mekler, Eva (1988) *The New Generation of Acting Teachers*, Penguin Books, NY.

Morris, Desmond (1967) *The Naked Ape, A Zoologist's Study of the Human Animal*, McGraw-Hill, NY.

O'Reilley, Mary Rose (1993) *The Peaceable Classroom*, Boynton/Cook Publishers Heinemann, Portsmouth, NH.

Palmer, Parker J. (1983) *To Know as We are Known, Education as a Spiritual Journey*, HarperSanFrancisco, HarperCollins, NY.

——(1998) *The Courage to Teach, Exploring the Inner Landscape of a Teacher's Life*, Jossey-Bass Publishers, San Francisco.

Pierce, Chester (1975) "Mundane Extreme Environment and its Effects on Learning," in S. G. Brainard (ed.) *Learning Disabilities: Issues and Recommendations for Research*, Washington, DC, National Institute of Education.

Richards, R. (2007) (ed.) *Everyday Creativity and New Views of Human Nature*, American Psychological Association, Washington DC.

Richtel, Matt (2010) "Your Brain on Computers, Digital Devices Deprive Brain of Needed Downtime," *New York Times*, August 24, 2010.

Rickard, Pamela (2010) Personal communication.

Ristad, Eloise (1985) *A Soprano on Her Head*, Real People Press, Moab, UT.

Santayana, George (1905) *The Life of Reason, or the Phases of Human Progress*, Vol. 1., Charles Scribner's Sons, NY.

Savio, Mario (1964) http://www.fsm-a.org/stacks/mario/mario_speech.html. Online. Accessed July 23, 2012.

Sebestik, Miroslav (1992) *Écoute* (film).

Shanley, John, Patrick (1992) "The Dreamer Examines His Pillow," in *Thirteen by Shanley*, Applause Theatre and Cinema Books.

Singleton, Glenn E. and Curtis Linton (2006) *Courageous Conversations about Race*, Corwin Press, Thousand Oaks, CA. Forward by Gloria Ladson-Billings.

Sontag, Susan (1966) "The Aesthetics of Silence," in *Styles of Radical Will*, Farrar Straus and Giroux, NY (pp. 3–34).

Stanislavski, Constantin (1949) *Building a Character*, Theatre Arts Books, NY.

Stein, Gertrude (1922) *Geography and Plays*, The Four Seasons Company, Boston, MA.

Tatum, Beverly Daniel (1997) *"Why Are All the Black Kids Sitting Together in the Cafeteria?" and Other Conversations About Race*, Basic Books, Perseus Books Group, NY (Introduction, copyright 1999).

Tompkins, Jane (1996) *A Life in School, What the Teacher Learned*, Addison-Wesley Publishing Co., Reading MA.

Tugend, Alina (2007) "The Many Errors in Thinking About Mistakes," *New York Times*, November 24, 2007.

Wallin, David J. (2007) *Attachment in Psychotherapy*, The Guilford Press, NY.

Wangh, Stephen (2000) *An Acrobat of the Heart: A Physical Approach to Acting Inspired by the Work of Jerzy Grotowski*, Vintage, Random House, NY.

——(2005) "Revenge and Forgiveness in Laramie, Wyoming," and "Reply to Commentaries," *Psychoanalytic Dialogues*, 15 (1): 1–16 and 47–56).

Wilder, Thornton (1938) *Three Plays*, Harper and Row, NY.

Wilkinson, James (1982) "Varieties of Teaching," in Margaret Morganroth Gullette (ed.) *The Art and Craft of Teaching*, Harvard-Danforth Center for Teaching and Learning, Cambridge, MA (pp. 1–9).

Williamson, Marianne (1992) *A Return To Love: Reflections on the Principles of A Course in Miracles*, HarperCollins, NY.

Winnicott, D. W. (1967) "Mirror Role of Mother and Family in Child Development," in *Playing and Reality*, Tavistock, London (pp. 111–18).

——(1986) *Home is Where We Start From*, W. W. Norton & Co., NY.

Zull, James E. (2002) *The Art of Changing the Brain, Enriching Teaching by Exploring the Biology of Learning*, Stylus, Sterling, VA.